OPPOSING VIEWPOINTS® SERIES

Domestic Terrorism

Other Books of Related Interest:

Opposing Viewpoints Series

Airport Security

Bioterrorism

Hacking and Hackers

At Issue Series

Biological and Chemical Weapons

Self-Defense Laws

Current Controversies Series

Gangs

Racial Profiling

Violence in the Media

"Congress shall make no law . . . abridging the freedom of speech, or of the press."

First Amendment to the US Constitution

The basic foundation of our democracy is the First Amendment guarantee of freedom of expression. The Opposing Viewpoints series is dedicated to the concept of this basic freedom and the idea that it is more important to practice it than to enshrine it.

OPPOSING
VIEWPOINTS®
SERIES

Domestic Terrorism

Margaret Haerens, Book Editor

GREENHAVEN PRESS
A part of Gale, Cengage Learning

GALE
CENGAGE Learning·

Farmington Hills, Mich • San Francisco • New York • Waterville, Maine
Meriden, Conn • Mason, Ohio • Chicago

HV
6432
.D66
2015

GALE
CENGAGE Learning®

Elizabeth Des Chenes, *Director, Content Strategy*
Douglas Dentino, *Manager, New Product*

For more information, contact:
Greenhaven Press
27500 Drake Rd.
Farmington Hills, MI 48331-3535
Or you can visit our Internet site at gale.cengage.com

For product information and technology assistance, contact us at

Gale Customer Support, 1-800-877-4253
For permission to use material from this text or product, submit all requests online at www.cengage.com/permissions

Further permissions questions can be emailed to permissionrequest@cengage.com

Articles in Greenhaven Press anthologies are often edited for length to meet page requirements. In addition, original titles of these works are changed to clearly present the main thesis and to explicitly indicate the author's opinion. Every effort is made to ensure that Greenhaven Press accurately reflects the original intent of the authors. Every effort has been made to trace the owners of copyrighted material.

Cover Image copyright © MWaits/Shutterstock.com.

LIBRARY OF CONGRESS CATALOGING-IN-PUBLICATION DATA

Domestic terrorism / Margaret Haerens, book editor.
    pages cm.-- (Opposing viewpoints)
    Summary: "Opposing Viewpoints: Domestic Terrorism: Opposing Viewpoints is the leading source for libraries and classrooms in need of current-issue materials. The viewpoints are selected from a wide range of highly respected sources and publications"-- Provided by publisher.
    Includes bibliographical references and index.
    ISBN 978-0-7377-7254-8 (hardback) -- ISBN 978-0-7377-7255-5 (pbk.)
    1. Domestic terrorism--United States. 2. Domestic terrorism--United States. 3. National security--Law and legislation--United States. I. Haerens, Margaret, editor of compilation.
    HV6432.D66 2015
    363.3250973--dc23
                                                                    2014019342

Printed in the United States of America
1 2 3 4 5 6 7 18 17 16 15 14

Contents

Chapter 3: How Might the Threat of Domestic Terrorism Be Averted or Prevented?

Why Consider Opposing Viewpoints?

> *"The only way in which a human being can make some approach to knowing the whole of a subject is by hearing what can be said about it by persons of every variety of opinion and studying all modes in which it can be looked at by every character of mind. No wise man ever acquired his wisdom in any mode but this."*
>
> *John Stuart Mill*

In our media-intensive culture it is not difficult to find differing opinions. Thousands of newspapers and magazines and dozens of radio and television talk shows resound with differing points of view. The difficulty lies in deciding which opinion to agree with and which "experts" seem the most credible. The more inundated we become with differing opinions and claims, the more essential it is to hone critical reading and thinking skills to evaluate these ideas. Opposing Viewpoints books address this problem directly by presenting stimulating debates that can be used to enhance and teach these skills. The varied opinions contained in each book examine many different aspects of a single issue. While examining these conveniently edited opposing views, readers can develop critical thinking skills such as the ability to compare and contrast authors' credibility, facts, argumentation styles, use of persuasive techniques, and other stylistic tools. In short, the Opposing Viewpoints Series is an ideal way to attain the higher-level thinking and reading skills so essential in a culture of diverse and contradictory opinions.

In addition to providing a tool for critical thinking, Opposing Viewpoints books challenge readers to question their own strongly held opinions and assumptions. Most people form their opinions on the basis of upbringing, peer pressure, and personal, cultural, or professional bias. By reading carefully balanced opposing views, readers must directly confront new ideas as well as the opinions of those with whom they disagree. This is not to argue simplistically that everyone who reads opposing views will—or should—change his or her opinion. Instead, the series enhances readers' understanding of their own views by encouraging confrontation with opposing ideas. Careful examination of others' views can lead to the readers' understanding of the logical inconsistencies in their own opinions, perspective on why they hold an opinion, and the consideration of the possibility that their opinion requires further evaluation.

Evaluating Other Opinions

To ensure that this type of examination occurs, Opposing Viewpoints books present all types of opinions. Prominent spokespeople on different sides of each issue as well as well-known professionals from many disciplines challenge the reader. An additional goal of the series is to provide a forum for other, less known, or even unpopular viewpoints. The opinion of an ordinary person who has had to make the decision to cut off life support from a terminally ill relative, for example, may be just as valuable and provide just as much insight as a medical ethicist's professional opinion. The editors have two additional purposes in including these less known views. One, the editors encourage readers to respect others' opinions—even when not enhanced by professional credibility. It is only by reading or listening to and objectively evaluating others' ideas that one can determine whether they are worthy of consideration. Two, the inclusion of such viewpoints encourages the important critical thinking skill of objectively evaluating an author's credentials and bias. This evaluation will illuminate an author's reasons for taking a particular stance on an issue and will aid in readers' evaluation of the author's ideas.

It is our hope that these books will give readers a deeper understanding of the issues debated and an appreciation of the complexity of even seemingly simple issues when good and honest people disagree. This awareness is particularly important in a democratic society such as ours in which people enter into public debate to determine the common good. Those with whom one disagrees should not be regarded as enemies but rather as people whose views deserve careful examination and may shed light on one's own.

Thomas Jefferson once said that "difference of opinion leads to inquiry, and inquiry to truth." Jefferson, a broadly educated man, argued that "if a nation expects to be ignorant and free . . . it expects what never was and never will be." As individuals and as a nation, it is imperative that we consider the opinions of others and examine them with skill and discernment. The Opposing Viewpoints series is intended to help readers achieve this goal.

David L. Bender and Bruno Leone,
Founders

Introduction

"Thwarting homegrown plots presents particular challenges in part because of our proud commitment to civil liberties for all who call America home. That's why, in the years to come, we will have to keep working hard to strike the appropriate balance between our need for security and preserving those freedoms that make us who we are."

—President Barack Obama,
Remarks at the National
Defense University, May 23, 2013

On the morning of February 18, 2010, a fifty-three-year-old software consultant, Andrew Joseph Stack, flew his small, single-engine plane into an office building that housed several federal government agencies in Austin, Texas. The crash killed both Stack and an Internal Revenue Service (IRS) manager named Vernon Hunter and injured thirteen others. The subsequent investigation of the incident revealed that Stack had planned the attack against the IRS office out of retribution for what he believed to be unfair treatment by the agency.

In a suicide note posted online, Stack poured out his anger with the US government. He also urged other Americans to rise up against what he believed to be an unfair political system. Despite the openly political tone to Stack's online message, the incident was not considered an act of domestic terrorism. Instead, authorities deemed it the act of a lone wolf with no ties to foreign or domestic terrorist organizations. The Federal Bureau of Investigation (FBI) classified it as a criminal attack on a federal officer—not a domestic terrorist attack. However, many noted that the incident seemed to fit the FBI's own definition of domestic terrorism.

Despite Stack's clear antigovernment ideology and intention to stir up opposition to the federal government's taxation policies, the attack was not viewed as domestic terrorism.

On the morning of August 5, 2012, a man named Wade Michael Page entered the grounds of a Sikh temple in Oak Creek, Wisconsin, and began shooting with a semiautomatic pistol. By the time the authorities arrived, Page had killed six people and wounded four others. After being shot by police in the stomach, Page killed himself with a shot to the head. The subsequent investigation into the horrific shooting found that Page had long been a white supremacist and neo-Nazi, but authorities found no suicide note or letter explaining the reasons for his crime.

In the aftermath, the Sikh temple massacre was widely classified as a hate crime or mass shooting. Without a clear statement detailing Page's motivation for the horrific attack, it could only be assumed that his racist and intolerant worldview played a major role in his motivation. Yet, some also perceived the possibility that it could fit the definition of domestic terrorism. At the memorial service, US attorney general Eric Holder called the attack "an act of terrorism, an act of hatred, a hate crime that is anathema to the founding principles of our nation and who we are as an American people." To this day, however, the Sikh temple shooting is regarded as a hate crime, not an act of domestic terrorism.

During the Boston Marathon on April 15, 2013, two homemade bombs were detonated near the finish line of the world-famous race. The explosions killed three bystanders and injured 264 others. A few days later, the FBI released video of the two suspects, who had concealed the bombs in backpacks, infiltrated the crowds near the race's finish line, and left the bombs to detonate in highly populated areas of Boylston Street. In a matter of hours, the two suspects were identified as brothers Tamerlan and Dzhokhar Tsarnaev, who lived in nearby Cambridge, Massachusetts. On the run, the brothers shot and killed a campus police officer and stole a car before engaging in a gunfight with police. Tamerlan was killed, but his younger brother, Dzhokhar, escaped. The next day, he was caught after a massive manhunt in the neighborhood.

During Dzhokhar Tsarnaev's interrogation, he confessed that he and his brother were inspired by extremist Islamic ideology and had planned the attacks to protest the US actions in Afghanistan and Iraq. Although the two men were self-radicalized, they had read terrorist literature online and had learned bomb-making techniques from an al Qaeda website.

The Boston bombings were regarded as domestic terrorist attacks before the suspects were even identified. Law enforcement officials later clarified that because the perpetrators detonated two explosive devices, defined under current statutes as weapons of mass destruction, the crime immediately was categorized as an act of terrorism. In an unprecedented move, the city basically shut down to aid in the police manhunt for the suspects: mass transportation stopped, thousands of police searched house to house, and the American public was treated to nonstop media coverage of the manhunt for days.

These shocking incidents—the 2010 IRS plane attack, the 2012 Sikh temple shooting, and the 2013 Boston Marathon bombings—are only three of the dozens that have occurred in the United States since the terrorist acts of September 11, 2001. All three have very different motivations, methodologies, and goals. Moreover, all three have generated debate on the nature and definition of domestic terrorism in the United States.

The debate over what kind of activity is classified as domestic terrorism is influenced by a number of factors. Since 9/11, a widely held concern is that too much emphasis has been placed on race, ethnicity, religious affiliation, and national origin. Are authorities more likely to deem an incident as domestic terrorism if the perpetrator is Muslim? Is it less likely if he or she is Christian? For example, why was Stack's suicide attack on the IRS office in Austin not classified as domestic terrorism? Why was the mass killing at a Sikh temple considered a hate crime rather than terrorism?

From another perspective, there are many Americans who believe that the media downplays domestic terrorism motivated by Islamic extremism and emphasizes violent acts committed by antigovernment zealots. They view attempts to study the problem of right-wing extremism as political correctness and deride the idea that domestic terrorism is a broad threat that can spring from different political or religious ideologies or social, economic, or environmental movements. In their view, domestic terrorism is mainly a threat that is inspired by Islamic extremist ideology, such as with the Boston Marathon bombing case.

The authors of the viewpoints included in *Opposing Viewpoints: Domestic Terrorism* explore the debate over the nature and definition of domestic terrorism in chapters titled "How Should the Domestic Terrorism Threat Be Assessed or Defined?," "What Groups Present the Greatest Risk of Domestic Terrorism?," "How Might the Threat of Domestic Terrorism Be Averted or Prevented?," and "How Should Domestic Terrorism Be Treated?" Other subjects explored in the volume include the efficacy of profiling to identify terrorist suspects, the necessity of protecting religious freedom and economic opportunity to fight domestic terrorism, and the best venue to prosecute domestic terrorist suspects.

 OPPOSING
VIEWPOINTS®
SERIES

 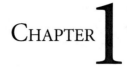

How Should the Domestic Terrorism Threat Be Assessed or Defined?

Chapter Preface

On the morning of December 14, 2012, a twenty-year-old man named Adam Lanza grabbed a gun from his mother's collection and shot her in the head while she slept. He then took his mother's rifle and drove to a local elementary school in Newtown, Connecticut. Only minutes after arriving at Sandy Hook Elementary School, Lanza shot his way into the school and began killing administrators, teachers, and students. As the police arrived, Lanza killed himself with a self-inflicted shot to the head. Tragically, twenty children and six teachers and staff were massacred at Sandy Hook that morning. It is one of the worst mass shootings in US history.

In the aftermath, a grieving nation looked for answers as to why such a tragedy could happen. The media quickly launched investigations into Lanza's emotional and mental state, his obsession with violent video games, his mother's love of guns, and other warning signs of the impending attack. School security became a hot topic, and efforts were made in a number of American communities to better protect schools from mass shooters. There was an eruption of consternation over Lanza's ability to gain access to such a powerful rifle, despite his clear emotional and mental issues. As in the aftermath of every mass shooting in the United States, the national debate over gun control raged, leading to an attempt to tighten national gun control laws and protect vulnerable students from gun violence.

As the national conversation in the wake of Sandy Hook largely focused on issues of gun control, gun rights, and the connection between both of those and mental health, others in the media and government began to question the public's perception of mass school shootings. The collective grief and anxiety experienced by most Americans led some people to ask why mass school shootings were not regarded as acts of domestic terrorism. They asked why the perpetrators of such acts were immediately classified as "lone shooters," a category that allows the American public to dismiss school shootings as aberrations carried out by mentally ill malcontents, and not part of a larger trend of school shootings meant to intimidate the American public. If Adam Lanza carried out the Sandy Hook massacre to inflict mass anxiety, sorrow, and grief on the American people, shouldn't that be viewed as a form of domestic terrorism?

However, many commentators pointed to the current definition of domestic terrorism under the USA PATRIOT Act, which dictates that it should "(A) involve acts dangerous to human life that are a violation of the criminal laws of the United States or any State; (B) appear to be intended—(i) to intimidate or coerce a civilian population; (ii) to influence the policy of a government by intimidation or coercion; or (iii) to affect the conduct of a government by mass destruction, assassination, or kidnapping; and (C) occur primarily within the territorial jurisdiction of the United States."

If it were terrorism, these commentators argue, then Lanza would have identified his motive to elicit a particular emotional or policy reaction. Under the existing definition of domestic terrorism, therefore, mass school shootings, such as the tragedy at Sandy Hook, should not be considered anything other than the work of a deranged lone perpetrator with no known political or ideological motive.

The debate over school shootings and domestic terrorism is relevant to the focus of the following chapter, which examines how the domestic terrorism threat in the United States should be assessed and defined. Other viewpoints included in the chapter explore the definition of domestic terrorism; the nature of the threat; and the perception of domestic terrorism by the media, the federal government, and the American public.

> *"Focusing only on terrorism perpetrated by American Muslims misrepresents the scope and nature of domestic terrorism in the United States."*

Homegrown Terror Isn't Just Islamist

Risa Brooks

Risa Brooks is an author and assistant professor in the Department of Political Science at Marquette University. In the following viewpoint, she asserts that Americans must recognize the diverse nature of the domestic terrorism they face. Brooks points out that since the terrorist attacks of September 11, 2001, Americans have been primarily focused on terrorist threats from militants inspired by an extremist Islamic ideology. This focus is shortsighted, because it neglects a range of other violent and dangerous threats, including terrorists inspired by right-wing or left-wing extremism. Brooks concludes that a comprehensive threat assessment that takes into consideration the full range of domestic terrorism risks will ensure that intelligence and law enforcement personnel remain vigilant in their fight to protect all Americans.

As you read, consider the following questions:

1. According to the Southern Poverty Law Center, how many terrorist plots against the United States were hatched by right-wing extremists from 2009 through November 2011?

2. How many terrorist attacks were planned by violent anti-US-government militants between 1999 and 2009, according to a study by the Institute for Homeland Security Solutions?

3. How many terrorist plots does Brooks find were undertaken by homegrown Islamic extremists in the decade after September 11, 2001?

Monday's [April 30, 2012] arrest of five men accused of aiming to bomb an Ohio bridge raises disturbing questions about the attraction to violence of some contemporary anarchists. But it also offers critical lessons to Americans about the nature of the domestic terrorist threat they face—a threat more diverse in its ideological origins than commonly appreciated.

Since 9/11 [referring to the September 11, 2001, terrorist attacks on the United States] the country has been concerned primarily with terrorist threats from militants inspired by a violent jihadist ideology, like that associated with al Qaeda. In recent years fears have focused on Muslim "homegrown" terrorism, which typically involves plots in the United States initiated by American residents and citizens who are inspired by jihadi ideology, but lack formal connections to al Qaeda or foreign militant organizations.

Muslim homegrown terrorists may draw the attention of a nation still traumatized by 9/11, but such plots are no more numerous or serious than those perpetrated by other domestic terrorists in the United States. As the country's history and Monday's arrests underscore, extremism comes in many incarnations. Focusing only on terrorism perpetrated by American Muslims misrepresents the scope and nature of domestic terrorism in the United States. It risks leaving us vulnerable to attacks from other sorts of violent ideologues and promotes a hurtful—and pointless—tension between Muslim Americans and other Americans.

A Long History of Domestic Terrorism

There have been many instances of non-jihadist terror in the U.S. Some may recall that in the late 1960s and 1970s the country faced an onslaught of bombings and attacks by social revolutionary groups and Puerto Rican nationalists. That violent era eventually ebbed, but then in the 1980s and 1990s the country witnessed an upsurge of threats from right-wing militants.

While Timothy McVeigh's 1995 bombing of the Alfred P. Murrah Federal Building in Oklahoma City was unusual in its lethality, it was unfortunately far from the only plot hatched by extremists on the right. The Southern Poverty Law Center documents 75 plots, of varying degrees of operational advancement, between July 1995 and June 2009 and an additional 22 from 2009 through November 2011.

A study by the Institute for Homeland Security Solutions, a research consortium in North Carolina, found that from 1999–2009, in the United States there were 17 al Qaeda–inspired plots undertaken, 20 plots initiated by white supremacists and 17 by violent antigovernment militants. Recent attacks include the 2009 shooting of a guard at the U.S. Holocaust Memorial Museum and the murder by "sovereign citizens" in 2010 of two Arkansas police officers at a traffic stop. In January 2011, a bomb laced with rat poison was found in a backpack along the route of a Martin Luther King Jr. parade in Spokane, Washington.

Ecoterrorists and animal rights activists too have perpetrated their share of bombings and attacks in the United States,

© Rick McKee/Cagle Cartoons Inc.

especially in the last decade. While these groups aim to avoid civilian deaths, accidents can happen and produce sobering acts of violence.

Homegrown Jihadists

Add to the mix militants inspired by jihadist ideology. In the decade following 9/11, by my own accounting, there have been 18 plots in which militants have taken at least some preliminary operational steps to realize their deadly mission. Like the alleged anarchist attack, 12 have involved informants and federal agents whose presence can help advance plots that otherwise may have remained aspirational.

All but two of these plots have failed or been foiled by law enforcement: Army major Nidal Malik Hasan's 2009 Fort Hood attack and a lesser known shooting, also in 2009, outside a Little Rock army recruiting center that harmed two soldiers. The perpetrators of all 18 homegrown plots had been known to law enforcement before their attempted attacks, with the exception of the May 2010 Times Square bomber, Faisal Shahzad, whose own failings as a bomb maker, despite hisoverseas training, underscore the challenges of successfully executing attacks in the contemporary United States.

The Need for a Comprehensive Assessment

Some may recoil at grouping right-wing, single-issue, and left-wing terrorists with militant jihadists. Yet, there are several benefits to promoting a more comprehensive assessment of the domestic terrorist threat. First, it ensures that society remains vigilant against threats from different subgroups and that law enforcement has the support and bureaucratic incentives to do the same. As Norwegians learned with the 2011 attacks by Anders Behring Breivik, neglecting the threat from the right (or other ideological extremes) can leave society dangerously vulnerable.

Second, focusing our attention on domestic terrorism of all types and not just that generated by Muslim Americans can help heal the social rifts generated by 9/11. Singling out Muslim militants when we talk about terrorism in the U.S. adds to the mutual alienation of Muslims and Americans of other backgrounds. By unifying in opposition to extremism of all types, we demonstrate to ourselves and to our terrorist adversaries abroad that we remain true to American values and principles.

"Well, you might be suspicious and a domestic terrorist if you purchase meals ready to eat, weatherproofed ammunition or match containers, night vision devices, night flashlights or gas masks."

The Definition of Domestic Terrorism Is Too Broad

Ms. Smith

Ms. Smith is a writer, a web developer, a programmer, and an expert on Internet privacy and security issues. In the following viewpoint, she warns that the US government has gone too far in its efforts to define and recognize domestic terrorists. As an example, Smith points to a 2011 Federal Bureau of Investigation (FBI) memo that offered tips to identify potential domestic terrorists that was handed out to military surplus stores, hotels and motels, gun shops, and farm supply companies all over the United States. According to Smith, the FBI's domestic terrorist indicators are so extensive that many innocent people could be classified as terrorists. As it stands, contends Smith, the FBI's memo is so wide-ranging that it should be regarded as useless in the fight against domestic terrorism and a threat to American civil liberties.

As you read, consider the following questions:

1. What US government agency does the author identify as having compiled a "Zombie Apocalypse" disaster preparedness list that was a viral social media sensation?

2. What social media sites does the author report that the New York City Police Department is monitoring for information on domestic terrorists?

3. According to the author, what US government agency has massive databases of secret watch lists?

You might be a domestic terrorist if you pay cash or if you "insist" on privacy when, for no reason, you are asked to show your identification. Sadly this is part two and *not* a You-Might-Be-a-Redneck-If-type joke as there is more proof that you might be a domestic terrorist if you actually believe your constitutional rights, or if you express concerns about Big Brother, or even if you have ever discussed the apocalypse online and your "radical" Christian beliefs. When it comes to disasters, if your plan is to "be prepared" like the Boy Scout motto, then guess what? Be prepared to be suspicious and end up on a watch list as a domestic terrorist. Prepared Girl Scouts are not safe either.

Oath Keepers [a group of former military and law enforcement personnel] posted a "communities against terrorism" brochure that the Colorado FBI [Federal Bureau of Investigation] handed out as a potential indicator of terrorist activities to military surplus stores. The alarming list suggests that suspicious activities include insisting to pay with cash or if the "suspect" demands "identity privacy." If you went into a military surplus store previously, don't alter your appearance such as by shaving, changing your hair color, or your style of dressing because that too may make you a domestic terrorist. Don't go buying items there as an intended gift because possessing "little knowledge of intended purchase items" makes you a potential extremist to be reported. Better shower well or use cologne/perfume because if you smell strange? You guessed it, you potential terrorist you.

That's not nearly all the "suspicious activity" that might get you labeled as a domestic terrorist. What if you are trying to follow disaster preparedness guidelines as suggested by other government agencies like DHS [Department of Homeland Security] or the CDC [Centers for Disease Control and Prevention]? Not too long ago, the CDC compiled a "Zombie Apocalypse" disaster preparedness list that was such a viral social media hit that it crashed the servers. Well, you might be suspicious and a domestic terrorist if you purchase meals ready to eat, weatherproofed ammunition or match containers, night vision devices, night flashlights or gas masks. *Examiner* journalist Kurt Hofmann pointed out that purchasing such items makes you a "suspected terrorist" but not purchasing the CDC's survival preparedness items means you will be devoured by zombies? Hofmann also says that ironically Homeland Security suggests that citizens have disaster preparedness supplies on hand.

Problematic Domestic Terrorism Strategies

It began when the White House announced a community-based approach to fight domestic terrorism and published "Empowering Local Partners to Prevent Violent Extremism in the United States." The strategy is to strengthen cooperation between law enforcement, communities and the federal government. Among other things, it will help "communities to better understand and protect themselves against violent extremist propaganda, *especially online.*" No big deal, you aren't an extremist? In what seems almost to be talk out of both sides of the same mouth, the document states, "Though we will not tolerate illegal activities, opposition to government policy is neither illegal nor unpatriotic and does not make someone a violent extremist." That is, it's *not yet* officially rubber-stamped to get your name on a watch list. While it recommends peaceful means, and I'm all for peace, we've seen how officially or not, members of peace groups have ended up on watch lists like they might be terrorist scum because domestic spying is nearly at Cold War levels!

Another White House proposed community-based strategy is a comprehensive gang model, but law enforcement has long been hunting for gangs and terrorists who utilize Xbox and PS3 [PlayStation 3] and warned the gaming realm like *World of Warcraft* is allegedly used to recruit and to plan chaos. Also, now the NYPD [New York City Police Department] has formed a new social media unit to data-mine Facebook and Twitter for mayhem.

"Under the logic of this most recent handout, the Boy Scouts should be reported as 'suspicious,'" wrote Oath Keepers. "Funny thing is, who exactly do the authors of these handouts think they are talking to when they ask gun store and military surplus store owners and staff to spy on their customers and serve as a network of government snitches?"

A Useless List

The flyers have also been handed out in Wyoming and similar brochures were passed out in gun stores from Utah to Connecticut. Authorities in Denver confirmed the suspicious activities document is "going to surplus stores, hotels and motels, farm supply companies that handle fertilizer and gun shops," Oath Keepers reported. "The answer to the government's silly lists is to make the lists so damn long they end up including every able-bodied American (who is supposed to be the militia anyway), and thus the damnable lists become useless."

According to WND [World Net Daily], a DHS Office of Intelligence and Analysis included "right-wing extremism" in the U.S. as "divided into those groups, movements and adherents that are primarily hate-oriented (based on hatred of par-

Definitions of Terrorism in the US Code

"Domestic terrorism" means activities with the following three characteristics:

- Involve acts dangerous to human life that violate federal or state law;

- Appear intended (i) to intimidate or coerce a civilian population; (ii) to influence the policy of a government by intimidation or coercion; or (iii) to affect the conduct of a government by mass destruction, assassination, or kidnapping; and

- Occur primarily within the territorial jurisdiction of the U.S.

18 U.S.C. § 2332b defines the term "federal crime of terrorism" as an offense that:

- Is calculated to influence or affect the conduct of government by intimidation or coercion, or to retaliate against government conduct; and

- Is a violation of one of several listed statutes, including § 930(c) (relating to killing or attempted killing during an attack on a federal facility with a dangerous weapon); and § 1114 (relating to killing or attempted killing of officers and employees of the U.S.).

"Definitions of Terrorism in the U.S. Code,"
Federal Bureau of Investigation, 2014.

ticular religious, racial or ethnic groups) and those that are mainly antigovernment, rejecting federal authority in favor of state or local authority, or rejecting government authority entirely. It may include groups and individuals that are dedicated to a single issue, such as opposition to abortion or immigration."

A Danger to Civil Liberties

You might be a domestic terrorist if you are a supporter of Ron Paul for president. Missouri law enforcement has been encouraged to report such suspicious behavior as having a bumper sticker that supports Ron Paul. A Missouri Information Analysis Center report also "warned law enforcement to watch out for individuals with 'radical' ideologies based on Christian views, such as opposing illegal immigration, abortion and federal taxes."

God help you if you are a hacker, in the sense of modding [modifying] whatever it is you plan to buy, cause that too is suspicious, you potential terrorist you. Although I'm joking so that I don't cry, I'm angry about all these &$#%*! ridiculous lists of what I consider innocent behavior being treated like it allegedly equals suspicious behavior. Guard your privacy and you are suspicious enough to be reported as a potential domestic terrorist? Why should a person be required to show identification if what they are purchasing is with cash and does not require ID? Homeland Security already has massive databases of secret watch lists! I'm a bit afraid to ask what's next. That online articles disagreeing with such asinine lists could be construed as civil unrest needing to be squashed?

"*[Political motivation] may be appro-priate for characterizing the violence in Syria or Egypt, but not in the United States, where terrorism is as likely to come from psychopathology and per-sonal gain as politics.*"

There Are Many Misconceptions About the Threat of Domestic Terrorism

Jack Levin

Jack Levin is an author, a journalist, and a professor of sociology and criminology at Northeastern University. In the following viewpoint, he addresses several misconceptions that people have about the character of domestic terrorism in the United States. Levin asserts that one of the biggest misconceptions the public has is that terrorism is on the rise, when the numbers show that the level of political terrorism has declined since the attacks of September 11, 2001. Moreover, most terrorism in the United States is homegrown, originating from right-wing or left-wing extremist ideologies, or single-issue activism. One of the biggest threats, Levin maintains, is from lone-wolf terrorists, who are not affiliated with any group and therefore are harder to detect and apprehend.

As you read, consider the following questions:

1. According to the author, how many men, women, and children did right-wing extremist Timothy McVeigh kill at a federal building in Oklahoma City in 1995?

2. How many deaths in Western Europe from 1950 to 2004 does Levin attribute to politically motivated terrorism?

3. How many deaths does the author attribute to the DC snipers?

The Boston Marathon bombers have brought a number of important assumptions into the national dialogue concerning the character of domestic terrorism. Unfortunately, the conversation has too often been filled with myths and misconceptions regarding the who, what, where, and why of terrorist activity in the United States. Four of these myths have been especially prominent:

Myth 1

MYTH 1: Terrorist attacks have increased dramatically since Sept. 11, 2001 [9/11]—so much so that we have reached a higher plateau where terrorism is the "new normal."

Actually, just the opposite is true. We haven't experienced such a low level of political terrorism in decades. The number of terrorist incidents in the United States, by the year 2007, was down to eleven. By contrast, there were many more incidents before the 9/11 attack on America—for example, 120 in the year 1975, 43 in 1982, and 48 in 1992.

Because of the incredibly large body count associated with 9/11, it is easy to forget the 1984 fatal shooting of outspoken Denver talk-show host Allen Berg by members of a neo-Nazi group known as "The Order," whose members raised funds through committing a series of robberies of banks and armored cars as well as counterfeiting. Or, right-wing extremist Timothy McVeigh's 1995 massacre of 168 men, women, and children at a federal building in Oklahoma City. Or, Eric Rudolph's 1996 murder of two and injury of another 150 in his bombings of Centennial Olympic Park in Atlanta as well as two abortion clinics and a gay nightclub.

Myth 2

MYTH 2: Most terrorism in the United States has an international origin and is committed by radical Muslims.

Actually, the majority of terrorist acts have no connections to the Middle East or Asia, but are strictly homegrown, originating with American citizens who are left- or right-wing extremists, animal activists, environmental radicals, anti-abortion extremists. Most are committed by American citizens. Few are Islamic fanatics. According to the FBI [Federal Bureau of Investigation], terrorist organizations in the United States have included the Animal Liberation Front, Aryan Nations, the Black Liberation Army, the Earth Liberation Front, the Jewish Defense League, Ku Klux Klan, the Order, the Symbionese Liberation Army, and the FALN (Puerto Rican independence organization).

Myth 3

MYTH 3: The United States has had more than its share of political terrorism.

Actually, the US has experienced dramatically less politically motivated terrorism than almost any other country in the world. Not surprisingly, terrorist fatalities are largest in countries such as Iraq, Afghanistan, Pakistan, Somalia, the Congo [the Democratic Republic of the Congo], and India. But even Western European countries have suffered more terrorist activity than the United States. From 1950 to 2004, for example, terrorists in Western European countries were responsible for almost 3000 deaths. During Northern Ireland's "troubles," some 1800 civilians lost their lives in terrorist acts.

In addition, there were horrific terrorist incidents in major cities across Western Europe. In 2004, for example, bombs placed aboard commuter trains in Madrid took the lives of 191 civilians and injured another 1800. In 2005, explosives placed aboard London's Underground trains and on a double-decker bus resulted in the deaths of 52 civilians and the four bombers. An additional 700 were injured.

Myth 4

MYTH 4: Terrorism is always politically motivated

The FBI sees terrorism, by definition, as having exclusively political motivation. This may be appropriate for characterizing the violence in Syria or Egypt, but not in the United States, where terrorism is as likely to come from psychopathology and personal gain as politics.

In 1981, John Hinckley [Jr.] attempted to assassinate then president [Ronald] Reagan, not because he disagreed with the administration in Washington, DC, but because he wanted to impress actress Jodie Foster with national infamy. His delusional thinking was enough for a jury to find him not guilty by reason of insanity.

In October 2002, the DC snipers held the residents of Washington, DC, Maryland, and Virginia in the grip of terror as they randomly shot to death 10 innocent victims. The snipers' motive was not to change national policy but to extort ten million dollars from the authorities in exchange for ending the slaughter.

The alleged Boston Marathon bombers, Tamerlan Tsarnaev, 26, and his 19-year-old brother, Dzhokhar, apparently came to identify closely with the cause of radical Islam, but that is not the whole story. These marathon terrorists were more like rampage killers who enter a school, cinema, or shopping mall and indiscriminately target anything that moves. Their motive for planting explosives near the finish line of the marathon seemed to be revenge: They apparently blamed the United States for wars in Afghanistan and Iraq, but they also seemed to blame everybody but themselves for their personal miseries.

It has been reported that Tamerlan was intensely angry—so much so that he disrupted a prayer service at his local mosque. The brothers' uncle referred to the two terrorists as "a couple of losers." And, it was true that Tamerlan had recently suffered some major losses. He had become unemployed, on welfare, and dependent on his wife's meager income. Moreover, the older brother claimed to have had no American friends and apparently did little better befriending fellow Muslims, being recently expelled from his mosque. The "final straw" may have occurred when Tamerlan, who was reputedly the best boxer in New England, was declared ineligible for national competition because of his lack of U.S. citizenship.

Referring to the Boston Marathon bombing, President [Barack] Obama used the term "self-radicalizing" to indicate the absence of an organized network such as al Qaeda.

The Lone-Wolf Terrorist Threat

In fact, many terrorists are no longer affiliated with organizations, even if they receive inspiration from them. Twenty years ago, the FBI was better able to infiltrate terrorist groups; nowadays, this has become—in cases where the terrorists are lone wolves or consist of a small "cell"—all but impossible. Since 9/11, the FBI has averted several potential acts of terror by their sting operations. On occasion, however, this tactic will probably be ineffective and the terrorists will succeed.

What can be done besides alerting our citizens to be vigilante? Somehow, we must reinstate the credibility of our public officials—our president, our Congress, and our Supreme Court justices—so that alienated Americans do not feel they must go outside of the mainstream and radicalize in order to satisfy their goals.

| *"Domestic terrorism in the United States is a cyclical phenomenon."*

Domestic Terrorism Is a Persistent Threat in the United States

Scott Stewart

Scott Stewart was a former agent for the US State Department and is a current analyst for Stratfor Global Intelligence. In the following viewpoint, he maintains that domestic terrorism remains a persistent threat in the United States and originates from distinct ideological streams. Although many continue to focus on Islamic extremism, the United States has a long history of extremist ideologies that radicalize into violence. In fact, the concept of lone-wolf terrorism and the leaderless resistance model of terrorist operations have been employed by extremist groups such as the Ku Klux Klan long before Islamic jihadist groups embraced it. Stewart argues that domestic terrorism is cyclical in the United States. It has peaked in recent years because of the intense political polarization in American culture as well as a wave of antigovernment feeling on both the right and left of the political spectrum.

As you read, consider the following questions:

1. According to Stewart, what political movement is associated with the terrorist attacks that occurred in Louisiana in August 2012?

2. What former Ku Klux Klan leader does Stewart identify as the mastermind behind moving the white supremacist movement toward a leaderless resistance model?

3. According to the author, who was responsible for conducting arsons at three Sacramento-area synagogues and killing a couple in the summer of 1999?

A string of incidents over the past month has served as a reminder that despite the intense, decadelong focus on the jihadist threat, domestic terrorism is still an issue in the United States. On Aug. 5 [2012], Wade Page opened fire on the congregation of a Sikh temple in Oak Creek, Wis., killing six and wounding [four] others. Though Page killed himself and did not leave any evidence explicitly listing his motives for the attack, his long association with the white supremacist movement was clearly a factor in his target choice.

On Aug. 15, Floyd Corkins shot and wounded a security guard in the lobby of the Family Research Council's office in Washington after the guard blocked him from entering the office. Corkins reportedly was carrying a bag containing a box of ammunition and a number of Chick-fil-A sandwiches. He apparently targeted the Family Research Council because of its public support for Chick-fil-A in the wake of the controversy over statements made by the fast-food chain's founder regarding gay marriage. According to media reports, Corkins said, "I don't like your politics," before opening fire.

And on Aug. 16, an off-duty sheriff's deputy was shot and wounded while working as a security guard at an oil refinery in St. John the Baptist Parish, La. When two other deputies responded to a nearby trailer park where a vehicle reportedly associated with the shooting was spotted, the trailers' occupants ambushed and killed the deputies. An additional officer was wounded, along with two of the suspects involved in the shooting, Brian Smith and Kyle Joekel. Seven people have been arrested in connection with the incident, including Smith's father and brother. News reports indicate that the group was associated with the sovereign citizen movement, and members of it were under investigation for weapons offenses and previous threats to law enforcement officers in other states.

All three of these incidents stem from distinct ideological streams: the white supremacist skinhead movement, the radical left and the Posse Comitatus/sovereign citizen movement. While unrelated as far as timing and motive, when taken together they show that extremist ideologies subscribed to by certain individuals on the fringes of U.S. society continue to radicalize some to the point that they are willing to take violent action in accordance with those ideologies. Domestic terrorism is thus alive and well.

Old Streams

First, we need to remember that terrorism is a tactic practiced by actors from a wide array of ethnic and religious backgrounds who follow various ideologies stretching from anarchism to neo-Nazism. Terrorism does not equal jihadism. Long before jihadism reared its head in the United States, anarchist Leon Czolgosz assassinated President William McKinley, white supremacist James Earl Ray assassinated Martin Luther King Jr., and Posse Comitatus member Gordon Kahl killed three law enforcement officers in a multistate spree of violence.

Indeed, as we look at all of the recent attention being paid to lone assailants and small cells, it must be remembered that antigovernment and white supremacist leaders in the United

States embraced the leaderless resistance model of operations long before jihadist groups began to promote it.

In 1989, William [Luther] Pierce wrote his novel *Hunter* [under the pseudonym Andrew Macdonald], which detailed the exploits of a fictional lone wolf named Oscar Yeager and was loosely based upon real-life lone wolf Joseph Paul Franklin. In 1990, Richard Kelly Hoskins published a book titled *Vigilantes of Christendom*, in which he introduced the concept of a "Phineas Priest," or a lone-wolf militant chosen and set apart by God to be his agent of vengeance upon the earth. In 1992, former Ku Klux Klan leader Louis Beam published an essay in his magazine, the *Seditionist*, that provided a detailed outline for moving the white supremacist movement toward a leaderless resistance model. Jihadists such as Abu Musab al-Suri first began to promote leaderless resistance only after the U.S. response to the 9/11 attacks [referring to the September 11, 2001, terrorist attacks on the United States] began to severely affect al Qaeda. But even so, groups such as al Qaeda in the Arabian Peninsula did not really embrace al-Suri's concept of leaderless resistance until late 2009, and the al Qaeda core did not follow suit until 2010.

A Familiar Pattern

The recent spate of incidents is also not all that unusual. Other examples stand out in recent years of different streams of domestic radicalism leading to a confluence of attacks by different types of actors. For example, on April 19, 1995, a large truck bomb built by antigovernment extremists Timothy McVeigh and Terry Nichols detonated outside the Alfred P. Murrah [Federal] Building in Oklahoma City, killing 168 people. Five days later, on April 25, timber lobbyist Gilbert Murray became the third fatality and final victim of Unabomber Theodore Kaczynski's long neo-Luddite [one who is opposed to modern technology] bombing campaign.

Domestic Terrorism: The Sovereign Citizen Movement

Sovereign citizens are antigovernment extremists who believe that even though they physically reside in this country, they are separate or "sovereign" from the United States. As a result, they believe they don't have to answer to any government authority, including courts, taxing entities, motor vehicle departments, or law enforcement.

This causes all kinds of problems—and crimes. For example, many sovereign citizens don't pay their taxes. They hold illegal courts that issue warrants for judges and police officers. They clog up the court system with frivolous lawsuits and liens against public officials to harass them. And they use fake money orders, personal checks, and the like at government agencies, banks, and businesses.

That's just the beginning. Not every action taken in the name of the sovereign citizen ideology is a crime, but the list of illegal actions committed by these groups, cells, and individuals is extensive (and puts them squarely on our radar). In addition to the above, sovereign citizens:

- Commit murder and physical assault;

- Threaten judges, law enforcement professionals, and government personnel;

- Impersonate police officers and diplomats;

- Use fake currency, passports, license plates, and driver's licenses; and

- Engineer various white-collar scams, including mortgage fraud and so-called "redemption" schemes.

"Domestic Terrorism: The Sovereign Citizen Movement,"
Federal Bureau of Investigation, April 13, 2010.

Another such convergence occurred in the summer of 1999. After conducting arsons at three Sacramento-area synagogues, brothers Matthew and Tyler Williams killed a gay couple in their home in Happy Valley, Calif., on July 1. On July 2, World Church of the Creator adherent Benjamin Smith began a multistate shooting spree that killed two and wounded nine and that only ended when he killed himself July 4. On Aug. 10, former Aryan Nations member Buford Furrow mounted an armed assault against a Jewish day care center in Los Angeles, during which he wounded five people before killing a Filipino-American mailman on the street.

Domestic terrorism in the United States is a cyclical phenomenon. There are discernable peaks in that cycle, like those we've discussed—and like the one the country is currently experiencing. The intense political polarization that has occurred in recent years in the United States, the widespread distrust of the government on both the extreme right and the extreme left, and the current election-year rhetoric will further inflame political passions. This means that the current cycle of domestic terrorism plots and violence is likely to continue for at least the next several months.

Implications

While domestic terrorism is currently at the peak of the cycle in the United States, it is important to remember that most domestic terrorism cases tend to be simple attacks conducted by a lone actor or small cell. There are far more instances of simple bombings, such as those conducted by [Centennial] Olympic Park bomber Eric Rudolph or animal rights bomber Daniel Andreas San Diego, than the sort of large truck bomb attack committed by McVeigh and Nichols, which was an anomaly. Even more common than bombing attacks are the armed assaults that we've seen recently, and they are generally implemented against soft targets—something we've talked about in relation to other terrorist threats.

And that means that the implications for domestic terror-ist threats are essentially the same as they are for the jihadist or Iranian threat. First, it is critical for people to remember that terrorist attacks do not appear out of a vacuum. Indi-viduals planning an attack—no matter what their motivation or ideology—follow a discernable cycle, and that cycle in-volves behavior that can be identified and detected before the attack is conducted. Indeed, it appears that the Smith family and their associates involved in the Louisiana shooting were known by authorities in several jurisdictions and were consid-ered armed and dangerous.

It is also important for individuals to understand that it is physically impossible for governments to protect all potential targets from every sort of attack. This means that many places are vulnerable to an attack, should an assailant choose to strike and should the assailant's preoperational activities go undetected. Therefore, citizens need to assume responsibility for their own security. This involves citizens not only report-ing suspicious activity to the authorities, but also practicing good situational awareness and having updated and appropri-ate contingency plans in place for their families and busi-nesses.

> *"[The] federal government must do more to combat domestic terrorism within the U.S. Our failure to act now will assuredly embolden the enemy and bring more attacks."*

The Threat of Domestic Terrorism Is Often Overlooked

Daryl Johnson

Daryl Johnson is a former intelligence analyst and the chief executive officer of DT Analytics, a private consulting firm. In the following viewpoint, he suggests that the national media and segments of the US government have overlooked the domestic terrorism threat, especially from extremist right-wing groups. In recent years, there have been several fatal and high-profile attacks from such groups. Johnson urges the federal government to recognize this growing threat because failure to act will strengthen these extremists and facilitate more attacks. Johnson concludes that there are several ways the US government can better fight the serious threat posed by domestic terrorism, including formulating a better definition of domestic terrorism; reinstating an annual report of domestic terrorism within the

Daryl Johnson, "Hate Crimes & the Threat of Domestic Extremism," Statement before the US Senate Committee on the Judiciary, September 19, 2012. Source: United States Department of Justice, 2012.

United States; providing the federal resources available to fight domestic terrorism; and offering quality training for intelligence and law enforcement personnel.

As you read, consider the following questions:

1. According to Johnson, how many attacks on US soil have been carried out by Muslim extremists since September 11, 2001?

2. When does the author say that the FBI stopped publishing the annual report "Terrorism in the United States"?

3. What federal agency does the author identify as having done a remarkable job training state and local law enforcement about the threat emanating from the sovereign citizens' movement?

The rising threat of domestic terrorism within the United States should not diminish our focus on deterring threats from al-Qaeda and its affiliates. Rather, our nation's intelligence and law enforcement resources need to be flexible and resilient in their ability to combat terrorism from all sources of violent extremism, including domestic non-Islamic extremists.

Today's Domestic Terrorism Threat

The threat from domestic terrorism motivated by extremist ideologies is often dismissed and overlooked in the national media and within the U.S. government. Yet we are currently seeing an upsurge in domestic non-Islamic extremist activity, specifically from violent right-wing extremists. While violent left-wing attacks were more prevalent in the 1970s, today the bulk of violent domestic activity emanates from the right wing. Recent acts of domestic terrorism have instilled fear within the U.S. population as extremists attempt to force their social and political agendas through violence.

Since the 9/11 terrorist attacks [referring to the September 11, 2001, terrorist attacks on the United States], Muslim extremists within the United States, either aligned with al Qaeda's ideology or other perverse interpretations of violent jihad, have carried out five attacks on U.S. soil. These five attacks resulted in 17 deaths (thirteen of these deaths resulted from a single violent act by Nidal Malik Hasan at Ft. Hood in November 2009). There have also been numerous arrests related to alleged Muslim extremist terrorists plotting in the U.S. since 9/11.

In contrast, there has also been a multitude of domestic non-Islamic extremist attacks—many of which have resulted in deaths and injury over the past four years. In particular, domestic right-wing extremists trumped all other forms of ideologically motivated violence in the U.S. for number of deaths during this time period.

Since the 2008 presidential election, domestic non-Islamic extremists have shot 27 law enforcement officers, killing 16 of them. Over a dozen mosques have been attacked with fire-bombs—likely attributed to individuals embracing Islamaphobic beliefs. In May 2009, an abortion doctor was murdered while attending church. Two other assassination plots against abortion providers were thwarted during 2011 and six women's health clinics were attacked with explosive and incendiary devices within the past two years.

Further, in January 2010, a tax resister deliberately crashed his small plane, which was filled with a 50-gallon drum of gasoline, into an IRS [Internal Revenue Service] processing center in Austin, Texas, injuring 13 people and killing a government employee. In January 2011, three incendiary bombs were mailed to government officials in Annapolis, Md., and Washington, D.C. Also, in January 2011, a backpack bomb was placed along a Martin Luther King Jr. Day parade route in Spokane, Wash. meant to kill and injure participants in a civil rights march. Finally since 2010, there have been multiple plots to kill ethnic minorities, police and other government officials by militia extremists and white supremacists in our country.

In August 2012 alone, a white supremacist killed six worshipers at a Sikh temple in Oak Creek, Wis. Sovereign citizens shot four sheriff's deputies, killing two, in St. John the Baptist Parish, La. And, four active-duty U.S. Army soldiers, who had formed an antigovernment militia group and were hoarding weapons and ammunition in an alleged plot to overthrow the government, were charged in the deaths of two associates who, they worried, might tip law enforcement to their clandestine activities. There was also what appears to have been an incident of left-wing domestic terrorism: a single-issue extremist shot a guard at the Family Research Council office in Washington, D.C. Unfortunately, these are only the latest manifestations of domestic non-Islamic extremist violence in the homeland.

It is also important to note that eight members of the Hutaree, an extremist militia in Michigan, acquitted this year of plotting to kill police officers and planting bombs at their funerals, had an arsenal of weapons at their disposal that was larger than all 230+ Muslim plotters and attackers charged in the U.S. since the Sept. 11 attacks combined.

Mr. Chairman and members of the Committee [the Senate Committee on the Judiciary], the federal government must do more to combat domestic terrorism within the U.S. Our failure to act now will assuredly embolden the enemy and bring more attacks.

Extremist Landscape in America

Violent extremism is a growing threat in the United States. The threat emanates from extremist belief systems that represent a broad range of religious, political and social causes. In particular, several factors contribute to the recent rise in violent antigovernment extremism in the United States: the economic recession, divisive political and social issues, shifting demographics in America and some policy changes endorsed by the new presidential administration.

Extremism is perpetuated through the words and actions of individuals, groups and movements—sometimes it transcends peaceful, law-abiding and constitutionally protected activity and includes threatening, criminal and violent actions. Some forms of extremism are successfully portrayed as acceptable, normal or even mainstream behavior, which can be deceptive and seductive. Adherents of extremism may also attempt to downplay and distance themselves from any negative stereotypes.

Of course, it is important to note that an individual holding extremist views, no matter how offensive, is protected by our Constitution unless and until he or she acts upon these beliefs by engaging in criminal conduct. Extremist belief systems represent a broad range of religious, political and social causes. On the far right of the political spectrum, right-wing extremists include white supremacists, sovereign citizens, . . . paramilitary and militia groups, and other types of antigovernment extremists. . . . On the far left of the political spectrum, left-wing extremists today are primarily comprised of anarchists . . . , black nationalists . . . , and some fringe elements of the Occupy Wall Street movement. There are also single-issue extremists representing both extreme ends of the political spectrum. Single-issue extremists are distinct from the other extremist types because they are overwhelmingly focused on a single political or social cause. On the far right, single-issue extremists focus their attention on targets related to abortion, illegal immigration or federal income tax issues. On the far left, single-issue extremists direct their interests against targets dealing with the environment (i.e., earth rights), animal liberation or antiwar causes.

I often describe extremist ideology in my law enforcement training as "a poison" absorbed into a person's mind. Extremist ideology uses deception, half-truths, and blatantly false and often over simplistic explanations to solve complex national issues or personal problems. Extremist ideologies are quick to blame others for these problems—often providing justification for violence and criminal activity. Scapegoats are also given (people, organizations and institutions), providing a lengthy list of potential targets to avenge these grievances.

Many right-wing extremists, particularly militia members, also perceive any mention of gun control legislation as a threat to their right to bear arms and, in response, have increased weapons and ammunition stockpiling, as well as renewed participation in paramilitary training exercises. Such activity, combined with a heightened level of extremist paranoia, has the potential to facilitate criminal activity and violence.

Current Limitations on Combating Domestic Terrorism

Domestic Terrorism Definition Confusion. The FBI defines domestic terrorism as "the unlawful use, or threatened use, of force or violence by a group or individual based and operating entirely within the United States or its territories without foreign direction committed against persons or property to intimidate or coerce government, the civilian population, or any segment thereof, in furtherance of political or social objectives."

This definition excludes violent extremists within the U.S. who are motivated by, or receive direct or indirect support from, international terrorist groups, such as al Qaeda. For example, Faisal Shahzad, a Pakistani-born American who attempted to detonate an improvised explosive device in New York's Times Square in May 2010, would not be considered a domestic terrorist given his alleged training by the Pakistani Taliban. Events similar to the Times Square attempted bombing are, therefore, beyond the scope of domestic terrorism.

Many scholars, media representatives and even high-ranking U.S. government officials misuse the term "domestic terrorism" to mean "any" terrorist attacks on U.S. soil (both transnational and homegrown terrorists). This is not an accurate use of the term "domestic terrorism."

The U.S. government's apparent misunderstanding of domestic terrorism was clearly illustrated as recently as 2010, when an antitax zealot chose to end his tax grievance with a suicide attack on an IRS processing center. In reference to this incident, DHS [Department of Homeland Security] secretary Janet Napolitano made public statements explaining that [Andrew Joseph] Stack "used a terrorist tactic . . . but he's not necessarily a member of a terrorist group. . . . This is an individual who had his own personal issues and personal motives. . . . He used that [the attack] as a means of carrying out a personal agenda." The Federal Bureau of Investigation [FBI] never publicly disclosed whether or not this incident was an act of terrorism. And, the 111th Congress passed House Resolution 1127 (H.R. 1127) declaring the attack on the IRS processing center to be "an act of domestic terrorism." Three different answers about the incident from different U.S. government institutions is confusing.

No Annual Report for Domestic Terrorism. While the National Counterterrorism Center and U.S. Department of State provide the law enforcement and intelligence communities with an annual summary of worldwide terrorism, there is no annual report summarizing domestic terrorism within the United States. Between 1980 to 2005, the FBI published an annual report entitled "Terrorism in the United States" which was released to the public. This annual report included reviews of domestic terrorism incidents, attempts and preventions. It was full of statistical information (tables, graphs and charts), policy information related to domestic terrorism, legislative actions, terrorism trends, FBI initiatives, among other valuable information. For reasons unknown, the FBI ceased publishing this report in 2006. The last edition covered a three-year time period (2002–2005) and was somewhat outdated when released. This annual publication was an extremely valuable tool not only for law enforcement, but also for academia, media outlets and the general public. This publication should be revived.

Lack of National-Level Resources. At the federal level, there is a shortage of analysts assigned to monitor and assess domestic extremist activity within the U.S. Currently, the FBI is the only federal agency that has devoted multiple full-time resources to research and analyze domestic terrorist tactics, tradecraft, and emerging trends. I commend the FBI's efforts to investigate and prevent acts of domestic terrorism. Nevertheless, as a law enforcement agency, the FBI is limited to its law enforcement mission, which mandates establishing "probable cause" or "reasonable suspicion" of criminal activity prior to collecting, analyzing and retaining information pertaining to domestic extremist activity. Further, the FBI appears to limit its domestic terrorism analysis to FBI case information only. These limitations impact the U.S. government's ability to forecast and warn of domestic terrorist activity before it happens.

While employed at DHS, I oversaw the work of five analysts responsible for analyzing domestic extremist activity in the U.S. This team was recently disbanded—leaving a single analyst at I&A [Office of Intelligence and Analysis] responsible for monitoring the entire spectrum of domestic non-Islamic extremism at a vulnerable time of heightened extremist activity throughout the country.

Other federal law enforcement agencies, such as the U.S. Secret Service, U.S. Capitol Police, U.S. Marshals, and ATF [Bureau of Alcohol, Tobacco, Firearms and Explosives], have limited resources to monitor various aspects of domestic terrorism, such as threats against political figures, counterfeiting, judicial threats, firearms and explosives violations, etc. Most of these resources consist of a single analyst at each agency devoted part-time or on an "as needed" basis to this subject.

Many federal law enforcement agencies have also adopted a universal approach to intelligence analysis—emphasizing expanded analytical portfolios in an effort to meet growing demands with limited resources. There is virtually no effort made to develop subject matter expertise (which takes extra effort and time). The "jack of all trades, master of none" approach to analysis negatively impacts the development of the necessary level of knowledge and expertise required to develop an in-depth understanding of the wide range and complexity of domestic extremist movements operating within the U.S. Further, federal law enforcement agency resources are more often tactically focused on active criminal investigations and providing case support (database checks, link diagrams, time lines, etc.), rather than conducting strategic intelligence analysis, such as reporting national trends, writing strategic threat assessments or analyzing extremist recruitment and radicalization. There should be a renewed focus on strategic analysis of domestic extremist activity.

Training Issues. Many law enforcement officers and analysts who looked at domestic terrorism issues during the 1990s have retired or have moved on to other assignments, which leaves a massive void in knowledge and experience. A whole generation of state and local officers has not been trained and has no clue what to look for. The Justice Department's Bureau of Justice Assistance (BJA) has done a remarkable job of training state and local law enforcement about the threat from the sovereign citizens' movement. This program, which began in 2010, should be expanded to include other violent forms of domestic extremism. Other agencies and organizations, such as DHS and its state and local fusion centers, should follow BJA's lead and develop similar training programs on domestic extremist activity. Perhaps those who have worked these issues in the past and have since retired can be utilized to educate and train the new generation of law enforcement officers and analysts.

Training in behavioral threat assessment is also essential to the identification of problem individuals—before another incident like the Sikh temple shooting occurs. The law enforcement community appears to have neglected this effective analytical tool choosing instead to emphasize suspicious activity reporting. Using the threat management methodology as a law enforcement tool has proven effective time and again—so why isn't it being used?

First, it's labor and resource intensive. During the 1990s, few police agencies were engaging in this method because of time constraints and lack of understanding. Today, however, we have available man power at state fusion centers, and we have available technology with pattern and anomaly-matching software. What is needed now is a better understanding of why this tool is important, and how it can help agencies to identify these individuals before they violently act out.

Second, along with training in identification and assessment methodologies, state and local agencies need training on how to manage these cases in the short and long term. The radicalization period for domestic terrorists can take days, up to several months or over many years.

Third, agencies need to liaison with their local mental health centers, district attorney, probation offices, and with the judiciary in their local community to make this an effective program. Such personnel may come into contact with an extremist through their work and could have additional information and insights worth sharing with law enforcement.

Lastly, handling these cases effectively calls for a joint effort and everyone in the criminal justice system must be on board and actively involved. This requires regular contact and follow-up between agencies.

Overemphasis on Suspicious Activity Reporting. It has been argued that law enforcement will never get anywhere in trying to stop ideologically motivated violence by looking at ideology

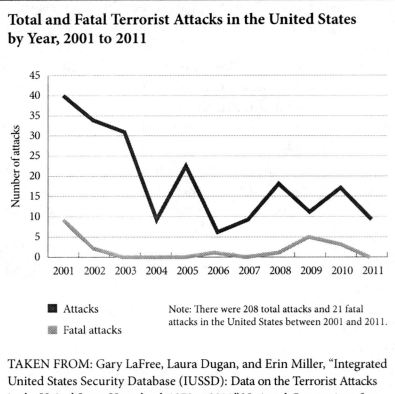

Total and Fatal Terrorist Attacks in the United States by Year, 2001 to 2011

■ Attacks

▓ Fatal attacks

Note: There were 208 total attacks and 21 fatal attacks in the United States between 2001 and 2011.

TAKEN FROM: Gary LaFree, Laura Dugan, and Erin Miller, "Integrated United States Security Database (IUSSD): Data on the Terrorist Attacks in the United States Homeland, 1970 to 2011," National Consortium for the Study of Terrorism and Responses to Terrorism, December 2012.

alone, because there are literally tens of thousands of individuals who are antigovernment extremists, sovereign citizens or racial supremacists (both white and black). Many others adhere to the extremist ideologies of the Far Left and single-issue causes. They might espouse violence, but not all act on it. In most cases, both the psychological factors and the extremist ideology must be present, along with some precipitating life event (which often serves as the catalyst to violence).

Conversely, those who are attempting to identify potential threats and prevent acts of violence should avoid looking exclusively at suspicious behaviors. It is too time-consuming and yields an inordinate number of "false positives." In fact, there are more innocent people being subjected to highly intrusive privacy and civil rights procedures under the ruse of "suspicious behavior" than if authorities focused on extremist belief systems that have a proven track record of inciting individuals toward violence.

Every day, at airports throughout the country, Americans are being subjected to invasive screening procedures that are intended to detect explosives, weapons, and possible would-be terrorists. Yet, not a single bomb has ever been smuggled aboard a domestic U.S. flight by a terrorist in recent memory. Many amateur photographers and young students working on their hobbies or school projects have been accosted by security personnel and had their photos removed. Few, if any, terrorists in the United States have been arrested in the act of conducting photography as part of their preoperational surveillance. These invasive screening procedures at U.S. airports and elsewhere should be scrutinized more and used more sparingly.

In other words, it seems pointless to be looking for "various types of suspicious behaviors"—they're everywhere! Something "suspicious" to one person might be totally acceptable behavior to another. What appears to be "nervous" behavior more often than not has a legitimate explanation, such as a preexisting medical condition.

Some civil rights and civil liberties organizations, particularly within the U.S. government, fail to recognize the role extremist ideologies play in motivating extremists to carry out acts of violence. As a result, they have severely curtailed monitoring efforts within our nation's law enforcement agencies. Monitoring a person's behavior becomes all the more clear when coupled with an understanding of extremist ideology. As a result, there needs to be a balanced approach to intelligence analysis and threat assessment comprising both extremist ideology and suspicious behavior. A balanced approach is less likely to intrude on the everyday lives of ordinary citizens and gives law enforcement and counterterrorism resources the best opportunity to identify extremists on the cusp of violent action—improving terrorism prevention as well as mitigating potential terrorists.

Selective Vetting of Intelligence Reports. At DHS, the most prevalent hurdle to timely dissemination of domestic terrorism related information is the Group of Six (G6) review process. The G6 review process was implemented at DHS in the immediate aftermath of the DHS right-wing extremism report controversy. It mandated that intelligence reports from DHS/I&A be vetted through six offices at DHS headquarters, which included the office of general counsel at I&A, the intelligence oversight officer, the DHS privacy office, the DHS office for civil rights and civil liberties (CRCL), DHS office of policy, and the state and local program office at I&A.

The G6 review process as it currently stands negatively impacts I&A analysis, because some of the changes in products seem to be made using standards that are in direct conflict with intelligence community analytic standards. G6 review can adversely affect an analyst's objectivity and political neutrality. The apparent purpose and intent of the G6 review process is to "screen" products for objectionable words, phrases or topics that are "politically sensitive" or perceived as "offensive" to certain groups of people. In other words, it has a "risk averse" approach to analysis. The major "choke point" within the G6 review process is CRCL.

The G6 review process impacts the timeliness and relevance of I&A products through a seemingly endless cycle of edits, revisions and comments that can last for several weeks or months. Some offices—particularly CRCL—have even sent conflicting opinions about certain topics or products, which further delays timely dissemination. Specific to products dealing with domestic extremists, CRCL seems to apply an additional level of scrutiny that results in multiple cycles of review and constant correcting. For these reasons, I&A stakeholders' needs are neither being met nor adequately addressed.

It appears that CRCL reviewers unnecessarily scrutinize domestic terrorism–related reports for more than what is within the scope of their responsibilities, such as questioning analytical judgments, source validation and source vetting. The G6 review process has called into question the reliability of credible sources of intelligence, such as various open source intelligence (OSINT) as well as information from reputable nongovernmental organizations (e.g., the Southern Poverty Law Center and Anti-Defamation League) without providing adequate reasons for these objections. I&A analysts have assessed reporting from such organizations to be credible and reliable. Furthermore, experts from these organizations have testified in trials as expert witnesses at the local, state and federal level. Other federal agencies (including, but not limited to, the FBI) have also cited these same sources that CRCL reviewers question or dismiss. CRCL objections related to using open source information impacts the reliability of products by withholding information from I&A stakeholders based solely on a risk-averse process.

Limiting Domestic Terrorism Analysis. Despite an attempt at developing a domestic terrorism production plan for 2010, DHS/I&A management chose to limit its analysis only to violent environmental extremists, violent anarchist extremists, and violent skinheads. As a result, I&A did not analyze threats from neo-Nazis, sovereign citizens and other violent antigovernment extremists. When questioned about the logic behind imposing these boundaries, analysts were told that violent environmental extremists, violent anarchist extremists and violent skinheads were the only domestic extremist movements to have attacked critical infrastructure in the past (identified as being clearly a DHS mission, implying that other domestic terrorist threats are not a Homeland Security concern unless linked directly to infrastructure threats). I&A management also explained that all three violent extremist movements were transnational in nature (which in their minds mitigated any intelligence oversight, privacy or civil rights and civil liberties concerns). They also rationalized that these movements had no history of infiltrating law enforcement (thus limiting the potential for future leaks). They went against the advice of domestic terrorism subject matter experts within I&A that this was not an effective way to analyze potential domestic extremist threats. I&A management's response had nothing to do with the level of threat or violent capability of domestic extremist groups. When challenged, I&A leadership decided to add violent militia extremists to the list but further limited this topic to illegal weapons possession and weapons stockpiling activity only.

Further, many reports dealing with domestic non-Islamic extremism produced by DHS/I&A during 2010–2011 did not appear timely and were primarily historical in nature. Few reports, if any, warned of emerging terrorism trends and imminent threats.

Periodical and Internet Sources Bibliography

The following articles have been selected to supplement the diverse views presented in this chapter.

Jerome P. Bjelopera — "The Domestic Terrorist Threat: Background and Issues for Congress," Congressional Research Service, January 17, 2013.

Benjamin H. Friedman — "Homegrown Failure: Why the Domestic Terror Threat Is Overblown," *Nato Review*, July 17, 2012.

Sumit Galhotra — "Domestic Terror: Are We Doing Enough to Combat the Threat from Within?," CNN, September 17, 2012.

Dave Gilson — "Charts: How Much Danger Do We Face from Homegrown Jihadist Terrorists?," *Mother Jones*, April 24, 2013.

Gordon Lederman and Kate Martin — "The Threat from Within: What Is the Scope of Homegrown Terrorism?," *ABA Journal*, July 1, 2012.

Sylvia Longmire — "When Is Mass Murder Considered Domestic Terrorism?," *Homeland Security Today*, August 21, 2012.

Dean Obeidallah — "Why the LAX Shooter Should Be Charged as a Terrorist," Daily Beast, November 4, 2013.

Brad Plumer — "Eight Facts About Domestic Terrorism in the United States," *Washington Post*, April 16, 2013.

Dawinder S. Sidhu — "Call the Colorado Shootings What They Were: Terrorism," *Baltimore Sun*, July 24, 2012.

Jeffrey D. Simon — "An Army of One," *Foreign Policy*, April 17, 2013.

OPPOSING
VIEWPOINTS®
SERIES

CHAPTER 2

What Groups Present the Greatest Risk of Domestic Terrorism?

Chapter Preface

In November 2012, the Combating Terrorism Center at West Point released a report, "Challengers from the Sidelines: Understanding America's Violent Far-Right," tracing the rise of the right-wing terrorist threat in the United States. The author of the report, Arie Perliger, underscored the need for a thorough and fair assessment of the threat to protect US national security. "In the last few years, and especially since 2007, there has been a dramatic rise in the number of attacks and violent plots originating from individuals and groups who self-identify with the far-right of American politics," Perliger observes in the introduction to the report. "These incidents cause many to wonder whether these are isolated attacks, an increasing trend, part of increasing societal violence, or attributable to some other condition."

Some of the right-wing groups examined in the West Point report include Christian fundamentalists, anti-federalist movements, skinheads and neo-Nazis, militia organizations, and antiabortion groups that have turned to violence and intimidation. The report found that although these groups exhibit diverse ideological beliefs and pursue different goals, they are all working to impose a far-right extremist view on the American public—and all of these groups have ramped up the violence to achieve their vision. "Although in the 1990s the average number of attacks [by right-wing groups] per year was 70.1, the average number of attacks per year in the first 11 years of the twenty-first century was 307.5, a rise of more than 400%," the report found.

Controversy erupted over the release of the West Point report. Conservative journalists and commentators called the report biased and motivated by an attempt to smear far-right groups as anti-American, deranged, and dangerous. Conservative journalist John Fund wrote in the *National Review Online* shortly after the release of the report that it read as if it were "laying the groundwork for a rhetorical attack on mainstream conservatism of the sort that President Clinton in the wake of the Oklahoma City bombing of 1995, when he blamed talk radio for stirring up anti-government passions. No one should be surprised if supporters of new gun-control measures begin justifying them by referring to the West Point report."

Some conservative commentators and journalists viewed the report as a deliberate attempt by the US government to downplay the true threat: Islamic extremists. Conservative author and blogger Pamela Geller in an article at the WND (World Net Daily) website alleged a government conspiracy. "This is another appalling attempt to demonize loyal Americans and whitewash the Islamic threat," she charged. "West Point is probably working on orders from higher-ups. Or else it has bought into the dominant PC [politically correct] culture."

Bill Wilson, the president of the conservative group Americans for Limited Government, took issue with the report's attack on anti-federalist groups. "As the Obama administration amps up its assault on our liberties, we must not forget that these intrusions affect Americans of all creeds and colors. It's also important to remember that taking a firm stand against these intrusions doesn't make one a radical, a right-winger or a racist—just an American exercising your right to free speech."

Defenders of the report argue that there is a legitimate need to study the nature of the right-wing terrorism threat because of the rising numbers of attacks from right-wing extremist groups. They contend that to study only the threat posed by the Islamic extremist movement would be a form of political correctness and would work to obscure the full picture of America's national security challenges in the twenty-first century.

The need for an assessment of the right-wing terrorist threat is one of the subjects surveyed in the following chapter, which examines the ideologies that have inspired domestic terrorism in the United States. Other viewpoints in the chapter consider the threat from Islamic extremism and lone-wolf terrorists.

| "We must stop these extremist invaders
| from raping the minds of American
| citizens on American soil."

Islamic Radicalization Is a Danger to US Security

Melvin Bledsoe

Melvin Bledsoe is the father of Carlos Leon Bledsoe, the perpetrator of a 2009 shooting at an army recruiting center in Little Rock, Arkansas, that killed one soldier and wounded another. In the following viewpoint, he traces the evolution of his son from a social young man to a violent, radical terrorist influenced by Islamic extremists to take up arms against innocent Americans. Bledsoe contends that Carlos was brainwashed by Muslim friends and mentors to assume a radical ideology and to assume uncompromising religious and political views. Bledsoe urges US authorities to recognize the problem of Islamic radicalization and the dire threat it presents to national security.

As you read, consider the following questions:

1. According to the viewpoint, where did Carlos grow up?

Melvin Bledsoe, "The Extent of Radicalization in the American Muslim Community and That Community's Response," Statement before the US House of Representatives Committee on Homeland Security, March 10, 2011. Source: Committee on Homeland Security, US House of Representatives, 2011.

2. In what country did Carlos receive terrorist training, according to the viewpoint?

3. In what year was Carlos arrested for overstaying his visa?

Thank you very much for allowing me to come here and tell the country what happened to my son. This hearing today is extremely important to begin the discussion about the issue of Islamic radicalization in America and my hope is that this Committee [on Homeland Security] can somehow address this issue in a meaningful, productive way.

First, I would like to express my deepest sympathy to the family of Private William Long, and to the wounded soldier, Quinton Ezeagwula. I would like to talk about those complicit in Private Long's murder—the Islamic radicals who programmed and trained my son, Carlos, to kill.

Carlos's Story

I want to tell the American people and the world what happened to my son. We sent him off to college at Tennessee State University in Nashville, Tennessee, in the fall of 2003. Our dreams about his future ended up in a nightmare.

Carlos is my only son. He grew up in Memphis, Tennessee. My wife and I operate a tour company in Memphis, Tennessee, and Carlos started helping out with the family business at the age of eight. He loved talking to the traveling public; and he had a lot of fun interacting with the customers.

After graduating from high school, he wanted to get a degree in business administration. We thought perhaps he would come back to Memphis to run the business and give my wife and me early retirement.

After the fall of 2005—his sophomore fall in Nashville— Carlos came home that Christmas for the holidays.

We were sitting around in the family room, Carlos's only sister, Monica, her husband and I, having a normal conversa-

Islamic Radicalization

The FBI [Federal Bureau of Investigation] defines home-grown Islamic extremists as U.S. persons who appeared to have assimilated, but reject the cultural values, beliefs, and environment of the United States. They identify themselves as Muslims and on some level become radicalized in the United States. They intend to provide support for, or directly commit, a terrorist attack inside the United States. The threat from homegrown Islamic extremists is likely smaller in scale than that posed by overseas terrorist groups such as al Qaeda but is potentially larger in psychological impact.

Donald Van Duyn,
Testimony before the House Homeland Security Committee
Subcommittee on Intelligence, Information Sharing,
and Terrorism Risk Assessment, September 20, 2006.

tion about life in general. But at a certain point, Carlos and his brother-in-law, Terrell, got into a heated conversation about the Muslim religion. Then and later, we felt like Carlos's personality changed when we spoke about Islam. We thought maybe he had some Muslim friends in college and was offended by our comments.

The next time Carlos came home, we saw another side of him that we hadn't seen before. During the night, he took down all the pictures from the walls in the bedroom where he slept. He even took the Dr. Martin Luther King Jr. picture off the wall. We asked Carlos: "What is going on with you?"

A Muslim Convert

He replied that he is now a new convert to Islam and that everything he does from now on will be to honor Allah. We got very concerned: While he was growing up, Dr. Martin Luther King Jr.'s picture had always hung on his bedroom wall; but now he treated the picture as if Dr. King was nobody to him.

We asked Carlos not to take Dr. King's picture off the wall, but he took it off the wall anyway. This became a big concern to us. We went to visit him in Nashville because we wanted to learn more about what was really going on with Carlos.

We discovered that Carlos had dropped out of school, at the beginning of the 2005 fall semester. He was working a temporary job. He had gotten a dog while in college, and now we found out that he had turned the dog loose in the woods because he was told that Muslims consider dogs dirty creatures. I really couldn't understand how he could do that, because Carlos grew up with a dog in the house since he was five years old.

So my wife and I thought that something or someone was getting in his head and changing the way he thinks. It had gotten to the point where he had no interest in coming home, even for the holidays.

All of this was part of brainwashing him, and changing his thinking a little bit at a time.

Brainwashing

He had a job in Nashville, together with some Muslims, who would tell him that according to Islamic law, his employer had to let him pray at certain times of the day, regardless of what was going on at the job. As a business owner, I told Carlos that it would be very difficult for an employer to do this for all of his employees.

As the next step on his process of radicalization, Carlos was convinced to change his name. He chose the name Abdulhakim Muhammad. At this point, his culture was no longer important to him, only the Islamic culture mattered.

Some Muslim leaders had taken advantage of my son. But he's not the only one being taken advantage of: this is going on in Nashville and in many other cities in America.

Yemen

In Nashville, Carlos was captured by people best described as hunters. He was manipulated and lied to. That's how he made his way to Yemen. Carlos was hoping to go there for a chance to cross over to Saudi Arabia and visit Mecca, as he was taught all true Muslims must do at one time in their life. He was taught that he would get to walk on the ground where Prophet Muhammad walked be able to travel around the area. But these hunters had other plans for him. They set him up, telling him that he could teach English at a British school in Aden in South Yemen. This school turned out to be a front and Carlos ended up in a training camp run by terrorists.

Carlos's joining in with Yemeni extremists was facilitated by their American counterparts in Nashville. We have since discovered that the former Imam of a Nashville mosque, the Al-Farooq mosque, wrote the recommendation letter Carlos needed for the school in Yemen. We also discovered that the school functions as an intake front for radicalizing and training Westerners for Jihad.

From what I understand, the FBI [Federal Bureau of Investigation] had been following Carlos since before he left Nashville and continued to do so after he came back from Yemen. When Carlos was arrested for overstaying his visa in October of 2008, he was interviewed by an FBI agent based in Nashville even before the U.S. embassy was alerted about the arrest. According to the embassy, the FBI was alarmed about what they learned from Carlos. We wish they could have told us—his family—about what they learned. If we knew how serious his extremism had become, we could have put in every effort to prevent the tragedy in Arkansas from happening.

A Changed Person

When my son was arrested in Yemen, my family cried out for help in bringing our son back to America from our government. We got in touch with the U.S. embassy and the State Department. We also asked for help from our U.S. representative, Steve Cohen's office, and from FBI special agent Greg Thomason, who had been tracking my son since Nashville.

After our son was finally released and brought home to us, no one said anything to us about what might have happened to him in Yemen or what they may have learned that so alarmed the FBI agent who interrogated Carlos while he was in the custody of Yemen's Political Security Organization.

Carlos's experience in Yemeni political jail was the final stage of his radicalization. He was in there with true evildoers—hard-core al Qaeda members who convinced him to get revenge on America.

The Elephant in the Room

Something is wrong with the Muslim leadership in Nashville. What happened to Carlos at those Nashville mosques isn't normal. I have other family members who are Muslims, and they are modern, peaceful, law-abiding people, who have been Muslim for many years and are not radicalized.

I also have several uncles and brothers in the military. Our family has fought for the United States in every war since the Civil War. I have nephews who are currently in Afghanistan, as I speak, fighting for democracy and freedom for all Americans.

It seems to me that the American people are sitting around and doing nothing about Islamic extremism, as if Carlos's story and the other stories told at these hearings aren't true. There is a big elephant in the room, but our society continues not to see it.

This wrong is caused by political correctness. You can even call it political fear—yes, fear. Fear of stepping on a special minority population's toes, even as a segment of that population wants to stamp out America and everything we stand for.

I must say that we are losing American babies—our children are in danger. This country must stand up and do something about this problem. Yes, it's my son's tragic story you're hearing about today, but tomorrow it could be your son or your daughter. It might be an African-American child that they went after in Nashville, but tomorrow their victim might have blonde hair and blue eyes. One thing is for sure, it will happen again.

Time to Act

We must stop these extremist invaders from raping the minds of American citizens on American soil. Here in America today, there are people with radical Islamic political views who are organizing with one goal in mind: to convert our citizens and to turn them against the non-believers. This is a big problem now in Nashville, on college campuses and in the nearby area. Nashville has become a hotbed for radical Islamic recruiting.

Carlos grew up a happy-go-lucky kid. He always had a big smile on his face, and loved to crack a joke or two. Everyone liked him. He loved to play team sports like basketball and football. He loved swimming, dancing, and listening to music.

Today we have two families that have been destroyed. This could have been prevented. I would like to see something change so that no other family in this great country of ours has to go through what our family is facing now.

GOD HELP US! GOD HELP US!

"Our national security is a serious matter and requires us to look at facts rather than rely on assumptions."

The Threat of Islamic Radicalization Has Been Exaggerated

Faiza Patel

Faiza Patel is the codirector of the Liberty and National Security program at the Brennan Center for Justice at the New York University School of Law. In the following viewpoint, she asserts that because domestic terrorism is such a serious threat to the United States, the federal government should be very careful to make a fair and factual assessment of the threat instead of focusing on one community—the American Muslim community. Patel argues that the premise that radicalization is prevalent among American Muslims and poses an existential threat to the United States is inaccurate and based on flawed assumptions and stereotypes. She suggests that basing congressional hearings on these flawed assumptions and singling out an entire community undermines national security by alienating American Muslims, who have been very helpful in terrorism investigations in the past.

Faiza Patel, "The American Muslim Response to Hearings on Radicalization Within Their Community," Statement before the US House of Representatives Committee on Homeland Security, June 20, 2012. Source: Committee on Homeland Security, US House of Representatives, 2012.

As you read, consider the following questions:

1. According to Patel, what percentage of American Muslims are African Americans whose ancestors were Muslims who came over on slave ships or who have embraced Islam?

2. In what percentage of the terrorist plots that have been foiled in the last decade does the author say that American Muslims have provided essential information?

3. According to a 2011 survey, what percentage of Americans believe that the values of Islam are at odds with the American way of life?

On behalf of the Brennan Center for Justice at NYU [New York University] School of Law, I thank you for providing me the opportunity to present testimony this morning.

I am Faiza Patel, codirector of the Liberty and National Security program at the Brennan Center. The Brennan Center is a nonpartisan public policy and law institute that focuses on fundamental issues of democracy and justice. My program, in particular, works to ensure that our counterterrorism efforts are appropriately targeted to the threat we face and are consistent with our constitutional values.

Terrorism is a serious threat to our country. Our response must be equally serious and must be driven by evidence, not assumptions and stereotypes. But this committee's [Committee on Homeland Security] recent hearings on radicalization do not, in my view, rest on a firm factual basis. They proceed from a premise—which is contrary to empirical evidence—that "radicalization" is prevalent among American Muslims and poses an existential threat to our country. Moreover, they adopt a view of "radicalization" that treats religious belief as a precursor to terrorism.

These empirically flawed assumptions, when given the imprimatur of a congressional hearing, have concrete negative impacts. They undermine our safety by alienating the very communities who have helped law enforcement uncover and foil attempts at terrorism. By casting government suspicion on an entire religious community, they may have contributed to anti-Muslim sentiment among Americans which manifests itself in polls, an increase in hate crimes and employment discrimination against Muslims, and opposition to efforts by Muslims to build mosques and community centers where they can pray and impart their faith to their children.

American Muslims' Response to Radicalization Hearings

The family of American Muslims encompasses many diverse communities. Thirty-five percent of American Muslims are African Americans whose ancestors were Muslims who came over on slave ships or who have embraced Islam. Others are immigrants from countries as varied as Kosovo and the Philippines, who have come to the United States to build better lives for themselves and their children. Some American Muslims are secular; others hold tight to their religious identity. They speak a babel of languages, from Urdu to Arabic to Swahili to French. You can find Muslims in every walk of life and every profession. Given their diversity, it is no surprise that we hear many voices responding to this committee's radicalization hearings.

But one message is heard again and again: these hearings unfairly single out American Muslims for scrutiny. No less than 74 Muslim, Arab and South Asian groups have registered this objection. Their views represent the opinions of tens of thousands of American Muslims. Other faith communities, as well as civil rights groups of every stripe, also wrote to this committee voicing the same concern. A total of 77 such groups included these concerns as part of the record of the first hearing. They were joined by 57 members of Congress and the editorial boards of newspapers across the United States.

It should come as no surprise that American Muslims feel unfairly singled out by these hearings. The hearings proceed from the assumption—which is contrary to systematically collected evidence—that "radicalization" is prevalent among American Muslims and poses an enormous threat to our country. The second—equally faulty—assumption of these hearings is that someone who is particularly devout in his or her Islamic faith is well on the way to becoming a terrorist.

Unfortunately, these errors are not harmless. They have dire consequences for our society. When members of Congress select the community of American Muslims for scrutiny as potential terrorists, it encourages all of us to view them through this lens. And there is reason for concern about the impact: polls show deep-seated suspicion of Islam and Muslims; hate crimes and discrimination against Muslims are on the rise; and, around the country, Muslims seeking to build mosques and community centers have met with opposition based on fear of their faith.

The Threat of American Muslim Radicalization

The first of this series of hearings was titled "The Extent of Radicalization in the American Muslim Community [and That Community's Response]." Unfortunately, the hearing did little to systematically evaluate this very question.

To begin any discussion of this topic, one must identify what is meant by the term "radicalization." While the term is susceptible to many interpretations, in the years since the September 11, 2001 [9/11], attacks it is generally used to denote a process by which Muslims in the West become terrorists. It has both an ideological component and a criminal one.

The ideological component is, in essence, the adoption of "radical" ideas, which encompass a range of beliefs from a conservative understanding of Islam to objections to the wars in Iraq and Afghanistan to the view that violence is justified in furtherance of religious, political, or social goals. Obviously, some American Muslims do espouse "radical" ideas, just like some people from every religious faith as well as some who do not espouse any religion. But leaving aside, for a moment, the question of whether "radical" views can be used to predict terrorist violence, do we have any evidence indicating that "radical" ideas are at all common among American Muslim communities? On the basis of empirical evidence, the answer is a resounding no.

Polling by the Pew Research Center shows that vast majorities of American Muslims have consistently held the view that suicide bombing and other forms of violence against civilians are never justified. Another recent poll, this one by Gallup, shows that American Muslims are *most* likely among all religious groups in the United States to hold the view that attacks on civilians by individuals or small groups are never justified. At least 7 in 10 American adults from all major religious groups agree that such attacks are never justified, but Muslim Americans are most opposed, with nearly 9 in 10 rejecting such attacks. Both polls show that American Muslims generally hold a "very unfavorable" view of al Qaeda, and fully 92 percent think that Muslims living in the United States do not sympathize with the al Qaeda terrorist organization. This empirical research supports the conclusion of a 2010 RAND Corporation report that individuals turning toward violence would find little support in American Muslim communities. . . .

The criminal component of radicalization consists of actions in furtherance of a terrorist attack and can include activities such as recruitment, operational planning, and, ultimately, execution. Of course, any terrorist attack that is planned or executed on U.S. soil is a matter of great concern. But when we examine the extent to which American Muslims have actually been involved in terrorist attacks, we find that the numbers are by no means indicative of a wave of terrorist violence. A February 2012 report by the Triangle Center on Terrorism and Homeland Security shows a total of 193 prosecutions of American Muslims for violent terrorist plots since 9/11, an average of just under 20 per year. There were no deaths in the United States resulting from terrorism by American Muslims last year. According to the report, after a spike in 2009, terrorist plots decreased in both 2010 and 2011. As the Triangle Center report explains:

> Threats remain: violent plots have not dwindled to zero, and revolutionary Islamist organizations overseas continue to call for Muslim-Americans to engage in violence. However, the number of Muslim-Americans who have responded to these calls continues to be tiny, when compared with the population of more than 2 million Muslims in the United States and when compared with the total level of violence in the United States, which was on track to register 14,000 murders in 2011.

Empirical research is borne out by the evaluations of law enforcement professionals who deal with these issues on a day-to-day basis. In testimony before this very committee last month [May 2012], National Counterterrorism Center director Michael Leiter said that the prevalence of violent extremists in American Muslim communities was "absolutely tiny . . . a minute percentage" of American Muslims. And, as Ranking Member [Bennie] Thompson noted in an op-ed last year, local law enforcement agencies that were asked to identify terrorist groups in their jurisdictions placed Muslim extremists fairly low on the list, behind neo-Nazis, environmental extremists, and antitax groups.

In contrast to the empirical research and law enforcement experts, the voices expressing concern about radicalization have relied on anecdotes and subjective impressions. These anecdotes and expressions are powerful and understandably give us pause, but they are not substitutes for sound, fact-based analysis.

Using Religion as a Proxy for Terrorism

Violence and crime—whether inspired by an ideology or not—are properly a subject for government concern. But these hearings are not focused on violence or crime. Rather, they focus on how American Muslim beliefs (the "ideological" aspect of radicalization) threaten our national security. They perpetuate the notion that it is what American Muslims *believe* that leads to terrorism. This view is encapsulated in the "religious conveyor belt" theory, which posits that there is a consistent path that leads American Muslims who harbor grievances against our society or who suffer from a personal crisis to become more religious, then to adopt "radical" beliefs, and finally to commit acts of terrorism.

But, as the Brennan Center's report, "Rethinking Radicalization," demonstrates, the process by which people turn to violence is exceedingly complex—a fact that is recognized by social scientists, psychologists, counterterrorism experts, security agencies, and the Department of Defense.

An in-depth empirical study by the United Kingdom's security service (MI5), for example, found there was no typical profile of the British terrorist and that the process by which people came to embrace violence was complex. It emphasized that there is no single pathway to extremism and that all those studied "had taken strikingly different journeys to violent extremist activity." Fourteen years of research conducted at the RAND Corporation similarly suggests that "no single pathway towards terrorism exists, making it somewhat difficult to identify overarching patterns in how and why individuals are susceptible to terrorist recruitment." The 2010 report by the U.S. Department of Defense on Fort Hood likewise emphasized that it is notoriously difficult to predict violent behavior of any sort. "Identifying potentially dangerous people before they act is difficult. Examinations after the fact show that people who commit violence usually have one or more risk factors

The American Muslim Population

The Muslim population in the United States is projected to more than double in the next 20 years, from nearly 2.6 million in 2010 to about 6.2 million in 2030, in large part because of immigration and higher than average fertility among Muslims.

Within two decades, the United States is expected to have the 43rd largest Muslim population in the world (in absolute numbers), up from 55th place in 2010. By 2030, the U.S. is projected to have a larger number of Muslims than any European country other than Russia (which is expected to have 19 million Muslims by 2030) and France (which is expected to have 6.9 million Muslims in 2030). By comparison, the United Kingdom and Germany are each projected to have nearly 5.6 million Muslims in 2030.

By 2030, Muslims are expected to account for 1.7% of the total U.S. population, up from 0.8% in 2010. If current trends continue, Muslims may constitute as large a share of the U.S. population as either Jews or Episcopalians do today.

"The Future of the Global Muslim Population,"
Pew Research Center, January 27, 2011.

for violence. Few people in the population who have risk factors, however, actually [commit violent acts]."

The Department of Homeland Security (DHS) and the National Counterterrorism Center (NCTC) are the federal government's lead agencies to combat radicalization. These expert agencies have made public statements that recognize the complexity of the radicalization process. DHS secretary Janet Napolitano has acknowledged that "there is much we do not know about how individuals come to adopt violent extremist beliefs." In 2010, a group of law enforcement and community leaders advising Secretary Napolitano noted that the "current level of understanding regarding the sociology of 'radicalization' and 'extremism' is still immature," and rejected the notion that there are overt signs of radicalization. The NCTC, for its part, has specifically repudiated the view that there is a "model that can predict" whether a person will radicalize, mobilize, and commit violence.

In fact, the religiosity-terrorism connection is refuted by empirical research. The British MI5 study, for example, found that "[f]ar from being religious zealots, a large number of those involved in terrorism do not practise their faith regularly. Many lack religious literacy and could actually be regarded as religious novices." Another researcher's review of five hundred cases found that "a *lack* of religious literacy and education appears to be a common feature among those that are drawn to [terrorist] groups." Indeed, there is evidence that "a well-established religious identity actually protects against violent radicalization."

Despite this wealth of empirical and social science research finding no connection between religiosity and a propensity for terrorist violence, and despite the evidence that support for terrorism and actual involvement in terrorist activity are extremely rare among American Muslims, these hearings continue to unfairly focus on one faith and one community. This focus belies the promise of our Constitution that all Americans, regardless of race, religion or ethnicity, will be treated equally by our government. Looking at facts, rather than relying on assumptions and stereotypes, will allow us to put the threat of terrorism in the proper perspective and put an end to unfounded insinuations about American Muslim communities.

Impact of Hearings on American Muslims

The committee's hearings are also counterproductive. They drive a wedge between American Muslims who have traditionally been staunch allies in fighting terrorism and law enforcement agencies. Starting in the days immediately after the September 11 attacks, American Muslims have unreservedly condemned terrorism. They have provided information on about 35 percent of the terrorist plots that have been foiled in the last decade. Top law enforcement officials have stressed over and over again that the cooperation of American Muslims is critical to our ability to fight terrorism. The attorney general of the United States has characterized their cooperation as "absolutely essential in identifying, and preventing, terrorist threats." As the head of the country's second largest police department, Sheriff Leroy Baca, testified before this committee:

> "It is counterproductive to building trust when individuals or groups claim that Islam supports terrorism. . . . Police leaders must have the trust and understanding of all communities who are represented in their jurisdictions. The Muslim community is no less or more important than others. . . . Simply put, police need public participation, and to accomplish that, strategies such as public-trust policing need to be a priority in our Nation."

It is not only the notion that Muslims are all potential terrorists that alienates the American Muslim community. It is also the notion of "cooperation" that several witnesses at these hearings seem to embrace. Even those Muslim Americans who are admittedly law-abiding citizens are essentially being told that they are responsible for any Muslim terrorists in their midst, simply because they share a religion. Moreover, because the "religious conveyer belt" theory interprets signs of religiosity as potential indicators of a terrorist trajectory, Muslims in this country increasingly are being asked to report on the religious beliefs and behaviors of their friends and colleagues.

Understandably, American Muslims who are more than willing to provide information about potential criminal activity, and who have in fact done so routinely since 9/11, are offended by the idea that they must share information about their prayers and religious observances with the government.

The hearings also drive a wedge between Muslims and their fellow Americans. When members of Congress hold hearings about the "radicalization" of American Muslims and expressly place an entire community under the spotlight, it sends the message to all Americans that the government views this community as a security threat. And the public appears to be receiving this message loud and clear.

Since 2010, we have seen a rapid acceleration in divisive anti-Muslim sentiment, rhetoric and activities. Recent polling shows that anti-Muslim sentiment is increasing among the American public. A 2011 survey found that 45 percent of Americans believe that the values of Islam are at odds with the American way of life. Another study reports that a majority of Americans (53 percent) say their opinion of Islam is unfavorable, and a startling 43 percent admit to feeling at least "a little" prejudice toward Muslims (more than twice the number who say the same about Christians, Jews, or Buddhists).

The Treatment of American Muslims

These negative opinions play out in how American Muslims are treated. Recently released FBI statistics show that in 2010, anti-Islamic hate crimes in the United States rose by almost 50 percent over the previous year. Data from the Equal Employment Opportunity Commission (EEOC) show dramatic increases in complaints of anti-Muslim bias in the workplace. Muslims are approximately two percent of the American population, yet, according to the most recent data, complaints about anti-Muslim bias accounted for 25 percent of the total number of complaints received by the EEOC.

Perhaps nowhere are anti-Muslim biases more evident than in the increased hostility towards mosques and Islamic centers. The protests against plans to build a Muslim community center near the site of the World Trade Center in New York are well known. But they are only the tip of the iceberg. From Murfreesboro, Tennessee, to Bridgewater, New Jersey, the efforts of Muslims to find a place to come together to pray have faced significant obstacles. The Murfreesboro mosque faced a lawsuit alleging that it was not entitled to the protection of the federal law that ensures localities do not discriminate against houses of worship. The reason: Islam is not a religion entitled to protection. In Bridgewater, New Jersey, the Muslim community searched for years for a site to establish a mosque. They found and purchased a site and worked with township officials to develop a plan for the Al-Falah mosque. But after vocal protests from the community, the municipality rushed through changes to its zoning laws effectively preventing the building of the mosque.

The Justice Department's analysis of cases under the Religious Land Use and Institutionalized Persons Act (RLUIPA), the federal law that ensures that localities do not discriminate against houses of worship, shows that while Muslims make up only three-fifths of a percent of the American population, some 7 percent of the RLUIPA cases investigated by the Justice Department involved mosques. The report found that "nearly a decade after the attacks of September 11, 2001, Muslim Americans continue to struggle for acceptance in many communities, and still face discrimination." Indeed, the report indicated that this type of discrimination was on the rise, noting that almost half of the matters involving possible discrimination against Muslims that it had monitored since September 11 were opened during or after May 2010.

Some members of Congress appear to recognize the faulty premises underlying these hearings, as well as their negative effects on our security and on our relations with American

Muslims, and have spoken out against them. I want to take a moment to commend them, particularly Ranking Member Thompson, for their tireless efforts to ensure that Muslims are treated as part of the fabric of American life. I am here today to ask others on this committee and in this Congress to follow these members' lead and to reject the flawed and divisive approach represented by this committee's recent hearings.

A Vital Partnership

When anti-Muslim sentiment was displayed in the immediate aftermath of September 11, it might have been understood (although not excused) as a reaction to the devastation of those attacks. More than a decade later, such biases must be examined in the context of government actions that perpetuate fear of American Muslims. These hearings send the message that Muslims pose an inherent threat to our country. That message has been heard, and its consequences are borne by American Muslims as they go about their everyday lives. But that message is not based on a rational evaluation of the threat facing us or how it should be addressed.

Our national security is a serious matter and requires us to look at facts rather than rely on assumptions. The facts tell us that terrorism by American Muslims in the name of Islam is a real threat but not a widely prevalent one. The facts tell us that American Muslims are happy to be in this country and condemn terrorism and al Qaeda by enormous margins. The facts tell us that it is not possible to draw a straight line from espousing "radical" ideas to committing a terrorist attack and that being a religious Muslim does not make one more or less likely to become a terrorist.

We also know what works to combat terrorism. Research shows that more than 80 percent of plots were solved through rigorous, old-fashioned police work, and that is what we should be stressing. We should investigate individual behavior that suggests potential criminality, not entire religious communities. Empirical research, as well as the expert opinion of law enforcement officials from around the country, shows that American Muslims are vital partners in preventing terrorism. We should build on these relationships of trust to foster true partnerships, not tear them down by casting suspicion on an entire community.

And let us not forget that all Americans—Muslims, Jews, Christians, Buddhists, Hindus, and atheists alike—are committed to the security of our country and our country will be safest when we all work together toward this goal.

> "It's about time that politicians who are quick to talk about the threat posed by al Qaeda began paying attention to the shifting nature of the threats."

Growing Threat of Extreme Right-Wing Violence

Peter Bergen and Jennifer Rowland

Peter Bergen is an author, a director at the New America Foundation, and an intelligence analyst for CNN. Jennifer Rowland is a program director at the New America Foundation. In the following viewpoint, they suggest that American politicians and the US public should be paying greater attention to the growing threat of right-wing extremism and violence. In recent years, the trends have shown that right-wing violence is rising and terrorism inspired by al Qaeda or Islamic extremism is on the decline. The authors say that studies show that this disturbing trend of right-wing domestic terrorism can be traced to changing political and economic conditions, including the recent economic downturn and the election of the nation's first African American president, Barack Obama.

As you read, consider the following questions:

1. According to the New America Foundation, how many right-wing extremists were indicted for their roles in politically motivated violent assaults between 2008 and 2012?

2. How many people motivated by al Qaeda's ideology have been indicted by the United States on terrorism-related charges since September 11, 2001, according to the New America Foundation?

3. What percentage of right-wing extremists indicted by the United States since September 11, 2001, have been in the military, according to the New America Foundation?

On the evening of March 19 [2013], Tom Clements, the director of Colorado's prison system, was shot and killed when he answered the door of his home near Colorado Springs.

The slaying sparked a police chase that ended a few days later in Texas, with authorities finally killing the suspect, 28-year-old Evan Ebel, in a shootout. It was soon discovered that Ebel had been part of a violent white supremacist gang during the eight years he spent in Colorado prisons.

Clements was the latest victim of increasingly active violent right-wing extremists. While American politicians and the U.S. public continue to focus on the threat from jihadist extremists, there seems to be too little awareness that this domestic form of political violence is a growing problem at home.

A Growing Problem

From 2002 to 2007, only nine right-wing extremists were indicted for their roles in politically motivated murders and other types of ideologically motivated violent assaults. But between 2008 and 2012, the number mushroomed to 53, according to data collected by the New America Foundation.

Fifteen right-wing extremists were indicted in 2012—including six who were involved in a militia in Georgia that accumulated weapons, plotted attacks on the government and murdered a young U.S. Army soldier and his 17-year-old girlfriend, who they suspected were planning to rat out the group to authorities. Seven claimed membership in the antigovernment "sovereign citizens" movement and allegedly murdered two policemen in Louisiana. And two had gone on a murderous rampage the previous year, killing four people before they were arrested in California, where they told police they were on their "way to Sacramento to kill more Jews."

By comparison, in 2012, only six people who subscribed to al Qaeda's ideology were indicted on terrorism-related charges in the United States, confirming the trend of the past four years, which is a sharp decline in such cases that has been documented by the authors in previous pieces for CNN.com.

It's about time that politicians who are quick to talk about the threat posed by al Qaeda began paying attention to the shifting nature of the threats.

Interesting Trends

In comparing the two sources of domestic terrorism, it's striking that the jihadists charged with crimes were much less likely to have actually carried out a violent attack before they were arrested.

According to data gathered by the New America Foundation, 207 people motivated by al Qaeda's ideology of violence against American targets have been indicted in the U.S. on terrorism-related charges since 9/11 [referring to the September 11, 2001, attacks on the United States]. But only about 5% of those were indicted for their roles in violent incidents, whereas of the 139 right-wing militants indicted in the United States since 9/11, just under half had engaged in a violent attack before they were arrested.

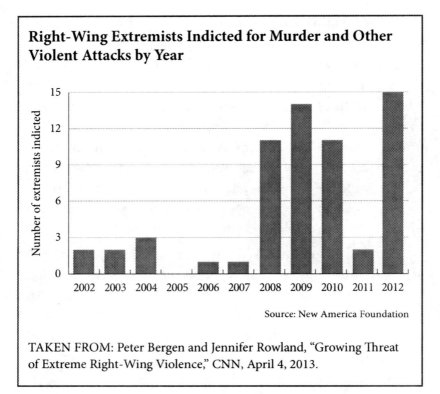

Right-Wing Extremists Indicted for Murder and Other Violent Attacks by Year

Source: New America Foundation

TAKEN FROM: Peter Bergen and Jennifer Rowland, "Growing Threat of Extreme Right-Wing Violence," CNN, April 4, 2013.

The word "terrorism" is not often used in the charges leveled against these right-wing militants, simply because laws in the United States primarily define terrorism as the work of a designated foreign terrorist group.

A True Threat

But the New America data show that domestic terrorists motivated by non-jihadist ideologies now pose a similar or even greater threat than those who admire al Qaeda. We define non-jihadist terrorists to be those who carry out or aspire to carry out acts of politically motivated violence, and who fall into the following categories: right-wing extremists who oppose the government, subscribe to a neo-Nazi ideology, or oppose homosexuality or abortion; left-wing extremists; violent animal rights activists; and violent environmental activists.

Over the past several years, acts or plots of non-jihadist terrorism have derived almost entirely from right-wing extremists like the soldiers' militia in Georgia and the antigovernment group in Louisiana. Of the 54 non-jihadist terrorists indicted between 2010 and 2012, 47 were right-wing extremists.

Seven were leftists or animal rights extremists. For instance, three were participants in Occupy Chicago, a leftist political movement, and were indicted on terrorism charges last June for plotting to throw Molotov cocktails at President Barack Obama and other officials during a NATO [North Atlantic Treaty Organization] summit in Chicago. Their lawyers say an undercover government agent had urged them to plot the attacks and build the firebombs.

Since 9/11, at least 29 people living in the United States have been killed by right-wing extremists, while 17 have been killed by jihadist extremists, the majority of whom died in one incident: the 2009 massacre at Fort Hood, Texas. Of course, this story would be much different if al Qaeda recruit Umar Farouk Abdulmutallab had detonated a bomb hidden in his underwear aboard Northwest [Airlines] Flight 253 on Christmas Day 2009.

But it would also be much different if city workers hadn't spotted a suspicious backpack left on the route of a Martin Luther King Jr. parade in Spokane, Washington, in January 2011, in which white supremacist Kevin Harpham had hidden a bomb packed with fishing weights coated in rat poison. Or if police hadn't discovered a napalm bomb and several other live, wired explosives in the suburban Cleveland home of right-wing extremist Matthew Fairfield in April 2010.

Chemical, Biological and Radiological Weapons

And of all the people indicted on terrorism charges in the United States since 9/11, no jihadist suspect has ever acquired or attempted to acquire chemical, biological or radiological weapons, while at least 11 right- and left-wing terrorists either obtained such materials or made serious attempts to do so.

In 2003, federal agents discovered "nearly two pounds of a cyanide compound and other chemicals that could create enough poisonous gas to kill everyone inside a space as large as a big-chain bookstore or a small-town civic center" at the home of Judith Bruey and her husband, William Krar, according to an Associated Press report. Alongside the arsenal of chemical weapons were about 60 pipe bombs, several machine guns, remote-controlled bombs disguised as briefcases, and anti-Semitic, antiblack, and antigovernment literature, the report said.

Although the feds had been tracking Bruey and Krar in the mid-90s, their case fell through the cracks when the events of 9/11 turned law enforcement's attention to jihadist terrorism. The couple was only found out when Krar tried to mail a package of counterfeit birth certificates to an antigovernment militia member in New Jersey, but got the address wrong. That mistake resulted in a tip to local police.

Right-Wing Terrorism in America

A report from the Combating Terrorism Center at West Point released in January found that, "In the last few years, and especially since 2007, there has been a dramatic rise in the number of attacks and violent plots originating from people and groups who self-identify with the far-right of American politics."

In a report that was much criticized at the time, the Department of Homeland Security predicted in 2009 that the nation's election the previous year of its first black president, along with a severe economic downturn that created disenchantment with the government among poorer populations, had the potential to radicalize greater numbers of right-wing terrorists. The same report warned that increasing numbers of returning military veterans as the wars in Iraq and Afghanistan wind down provided those on the far right with a vulnerable population to target for radicalization.

The New America Foundation data show that about 20% of the right-wing extremists indicted since 9/11 had spent time in the military.

The New America data support the Department of Homeland Security's assessment of the growing threat of right-wing extremist groups. American politicians and the public should become more aware of the fact that while the threat from al Qaeda–inspired terrorists is much diminished at home, the threat from right-wing militants continues to rise.

*"Over the last few years, the invariably
unjustified rush to pin violence on the
'right wing'—particularly the tea parties—has reached the point of parody."*

Right-Wing Extremists
Should Not Be Classified as a
Major Threat to US Security

Jonah Goldberg

*Jonah Goldberg is an author and a political columnist. In the
following viewpoint, he finds that the tendency to attribute recent domestic terrorist attacks to right-wing extremism is unjustified and bordering on absurd. Goldberg contends that these ac-
cusations emanate from liberal politicians and the mainstream
media because these groups are quick to conflate extremism with
the right wing. As a result, several recent attacks widely attributed to the right wing did not come from right-wing ideologues.
Goldberg points out that terrorists motivated by Islamic fundamentalism often get more of a presumption of innocence than
those associated with right-wing ideology.*

As you read, consider the following questions:

1. What socialist leader does Goldberg say had his prison
   sentence commuted by President Warren G. Harding?

Jonah Goldberg, "'Right Wing' Doesn't Equal 'Terrorist,'" *Los Angeles Times*, April 23,
2013. Copyright © 2013 by Jonah Goldberg. Reproduced by permission.

2. According to the author, who did Harry Truman run against for president in 1948?

3. What secretary of state does Goldberg state belonged to a group that once discussed assassinating American politicians?

"If history were to repeat itself," warned President Franklin D. Roosevelt in his 1944 State of the Union address, "and we were to return to the so-called normalcy of the 1920s, then it is certain that even though we shall have conquered our enemies on the battlefields abroad, we shall have yielded to the spirit of fascism here at home."

The "normalcy" of the 1920s that Roosevelt referred to was a time of peace and prosperity. The decade began with Republican president Warren G. Harding commuting the sentences of many of the people imprisoned under a sedition law during the [Woodrow] Wilson administration, including the socialist leader Eugene V. Debs. "Normalcy" meant the end to the Palmer raids [arrests conducted under the leadership of US attorney general A. Mitchell Palmer] aimed at rooting out Communists and other dissidents, the end of economic rationing, the cessation of domestic surveillance and the state propaganda of the World War I years.

Also, "a return to normalcy" was Harding's campaign slogan in the 1920 presidential election, which he won in a landslide over Democrat James Cox and his running mate, Roosevelt.

Roosevelt's Dirty Smear

That Roosevelt nurtured resentments against the Republicans for the drubbing he received in 1920 is no surprise. That those resentments ran deep enough for him to smear Republicans in 1944 with the "spirit of fascism" at the very moment we were fighting the real thing in Europe is nothing short of disgusting.

But it was effective.

Harry Truman recognized that when he ran for president against the liberal Republican Thomas Dewey in 1948. Truman charged that Dewey was the front man for the same sort of "powerful reactionary forces" that orchestrated the rise of [Adolf] Hitler in Germany.

When a Communist assassinated President [John F.] Kennedy, somehow the American right got the blame. Lyndon Johnson translated that myth into a campaign of slander against Barry Goldwater, casting him as a crypto-Nazi emissary of "hate."

After the Oklahoma City bombing, President [Bill] Clinton saw fit to insinuate that Rush Limbaugh and his imitators were partly to blame.

The Media

Such partisanship is hardly reserved for partisans. The late Daniel Schorr, then of CBS News, reported that Goldwater's planned European vacation was really a rendezvous with the German right in "Hitler's onetime stomping ground."

Schorr spent his golden years at National Public Radio. No doubt he would have been pleased with the "reporting" of its national security correspondent Dina Temple-Raston. Before the identities of the Boston bombers were confirmed, she said her sources were "leaning" toward believing that it was a homegrown "right-wing" attack, and cited that "April is a big month for antigovernment and right-wing individuals."

How so? Well, because April's when the Oklahoma City bombing took place, as well as the Waco siege, the Columbine shootings[1] and, how could one forget, Adolf Hitler's birthday.

---

1. The Oklahoma City bombing was carried out by Timothy McVeigh, who planted a bomb in a truck outside a federal building that, when detonated, killed hundreds of people and injured hundreds more. The Waco siege was a siege of a religious compound in Waco, Texas, by federal agents and Texas law enforcement that resulted in ninety-one deaths and numerous injuries. The Columbine shootings were a mass school shooting in Colorado that resulted in the deaths of a dozen students and one teacher.

Over the last few years, the invariably unjustified rush to pin violence on the "right wing"—particularly the tea parties—has reached the point of parody. Remember, when New York mayor Michael Bloomberg speculated that the foiled Times Square bomber might just be angry about Obamacare [referring to health care reform]?

Getting the Slander Right

As the *Washington Examiner*'s Philip Klein recently noted, among the myriad reasons conservatives take offense at this idiotic knee-jerk slander is that the term "right wing" is also routinely used to describe mainstream Republicans such as Paul Ryan and Mitt Romney. I can exclusively report that neither of them celebrate Hitler's birthday.

Every Muslim terrorist enjoys not just the presumption of innocence until proven guilty but the presumption that he's a fan of Ayn Rand.

Ah, but some would respond that "right wing" is different than "Muslim" because there's so much similarity between mainstream conservative ideology and the terror-filled creeds of the far right.

Except there isn't. Timothy McVeigh, an atheist, wasn't part of the conservative or libertarian movements. He wasn't even part of the militia movement. And what on Earth was right wing about the Columbine shootings?

Terrorism from the Left Wing?

In plenty of cases of multiple killings, from the Unabomber [real name Theodore Kaczynski] to Christopher Dorner [a former police officer who conducted a series of shootings of police officers and their families], the perpetrators espoused views closer to the mainstream left's than McVeigh had to the mainstream right.

And, recall that Secretary of State John Kerry belonged to a group—Vietnam Veterans Against the War—that once discussed assassinating American politicians. Barack Obama was friendly with a convicted domestic terrorist. But to even bring these things up, never mind invest them with significance, is considered outrageous guilt by association.

And you know what? Maybe it is.

But if that is outrageous, what do you call the paranoid style of liberal politics that has confused normalcy for fascism for more than half a century?

> *"The most significant domestic terrorism threat over the next five years will be the lone actor, or 'lone wolf' terrorist."*

Lone-Wolf Terrorism Is a Growing Threat

Jim Kouri

Jim Kouri is a writer and columnist at Examiner.com. In the following viewpoint, he offers an assessment of the security threats facing the United States in the next several years. Kouri contends that the most significant domestic terrorism threat in the next five years will be "lone wolf" terrorists, extremists who are ideologically motivated to plan and carry out high-profile attacks against individuals, organizations, or government targets. These individuals or small groups are extremely hard to track because although they are often inspired by the work of more conventional terrorist groups, they operate on the fringes of such movements. Other serious threats are posed by globalization, which will motivate more individuals to embrace violent ideology, and technological innovation, which will allow terrorist groups to improve communications and operations across larger areas.

As you read, consider the following questions:

1. According to Kouri, what recent event is an excellent example of the threat posed by the lone-wolf terrorist?

Jim Kouri, "Lone Wolf Terrorist Threat Increasing, Say Security Experts," Accuracy in Media, June 24, 2011. Copyright © 2011 by James J. Kouri. Reproduced by permission.

2. How does Kouri believe technological advances will make it easier for terrorists to stay ahead of law enforcement?

3. In the author's assessment, what is the threat posed by traditional left-wing terrorist groups?

With the Muslim world in turmoil, terrorist organizations are likely to find more and more recruits for their organizations. At times their recruits are unknown to terrorist leaders and commanders, but present a threat to nations throughout the world especially the United States and European Union members.

Terrorism is the most significant threat to our national security bar none. In the international terrorism arena, over the next five years, it's believed that the number of state-sponsored terrorist organizations may decline, but privately sponsored terrorist groups will increase in number.

These terrorist groups will increasingly cooperate with one another to achieve desired ends against common enemies. These alliances will be of limited duration, but such "loose associations" will challenge the government's ability to identify specific threats. Al Qaeda, and Hezbollah, and their affiliates will remain the most significant threat over the next five years, according to security expert Mike Snopes who runs a protection firm and served as a New York City police commander.

The Federal Bureau of Investigation forecasts that subnational and nongovernmental entities will play an increasing role in world affairs for years to come, presenting new "asymmetric" threats to the United States, according to a report submitted to the National Association of Chiefs of Police and other law enforcement and security organizations.

A Growing Role

Although the United States will continue to occupy a position of economic and political leadership—and although other governments will also continue to be important actors on the world stage—terrorist groups, criminal enterprises, and other non-state actors will assume an increasing role in international affairs. Nation-states and their governments will exercise decreasing control over the flow of information, resources, technology, services, and people.

The most significant domestic terrorism threat over the next five years will be the lone actor, or "lone wolf" terrorist. They typically draw ideological inspiration from formal terrorist organizations, but operate on the fringes of those movements.

Despite their ad hoc nature and generally limited resources, they can mount high-profile, extremely destructive attacks, and their operational planning is often difficult to detect. An excellent example of this is the lone gunman—a Muslim—who entered a Jewish center in Seattle and killed one woman while wounding five others.

The Effect of Globalization

Globalization and the trend of an increasingly networked world economy will become more pronounced within the next five years. The global economy will stabilize some regions, but widening economic divides are likely to make areas, groups, and nations that are left behind breeding grounds for unrest, violence, and terrorism.

As corporate, financial, and nationality definitions and structures become more complex and global, the distinction between foreign and domestic entities will increasingly blur. This will lead to further globalization and networking of criminal elements, directly threatening the security of the United States.

Technological Innovation

Most experts believe that technological innovation will have the most profound impact on the collective ability of the federal, state, and local governments to protect the United States.

© Dave Granlund/Cagle Cartoons Inc.

Advances in information technology, as well as other scientific and technical areas, have created the most significant global transformation since the Industrial Revolution. These advances allow terrorists, disaffected states, weapons proliferators, criminal enterprises, drug traffickers, and other threat enterprises easier and cheaper access to weapons technology.

Technological advances will also provide terrorists and others with the potential to stay ahead of law enforcement countermeasures. For example, it will be easier and cheaper for small groups or individuals to acquire designer chemical or biological warfare agents, and correspondingly more difficult for forensic experts to trace an agent to a specific country, company, or group.

In the 21st century, with the ready availability of international travel and telecommunications, neither crime nor terrorism confines itself territorially. Nor do criminals or terrorists restrict themselves, in conformance with the structure of our laws, wholly to one bad act or the other. Instead, they enter into alliances of opportunity as they arise; terrorists commit crimes and, for the right price or reason, criminals assist terrorists. Today's threats cross geographic and political boundaries with impunity and do not fall solely into a single category of our law.

To meet these threats, we need an even more tightly integrated intelligence cycle. We must have extraordinary receptors for changes in threats and the ability to make immediate corrections in our priorities and focus to address those changes. And, we must recognize that alliances with others in law enforcement, at home and abroad, are absolutely essential.

Weapons of Mass Destruction

The global weapons of mass destruction (WMD) threat to the United States and its interests is expected to increase significantly in the near term. We expect terrorists to exploit criminal organizations to develop and procure WMD capabilities. Globalization will make it easier to transfer both WMD materiel and expertise throughout the world. The basic science and technologies necessary to produce WMD will be more easily understood. Similarly, raw materials will be more available and easier to obtain.

Assessing the Threat

Violence by domestic terrorists will continue to present a threat to the United States over the next five years. The number of traditional left-wing terrorist groups, typically advocating the overthrow of the US government because of the perceived growth of capitalism and imperialism, has diminished in recent years. However, new groups have emerged that may pose an increasing threat. Right-wing extremists, espousing antigovernment or racist sentiment, will pose a threat because of their continuing collection of weapons and explosives coupled with their propensity for violence.

The threat from countries which consider the United States their primary intelligence target, adversary or threat either will continue at present levels or likely increase. The most desirable US targets will be political and military plans and intentions; technology; and economic institutions, both governmental and nongovernmental. Foreign intelligence services increasingly will target and recruit US travelers abroad and will use nonofficial collection platforms, including increasing numbers of students, visitors, delegations, and émigrés within the United States.

Foreign intelligence activities are likely to be increasingly characterized by the use of sophisticated and secure communication technology to handle recruited agents and to be more likely than in the past to occur almost anywhere in the United States.

> *"The lone-wolf threat is nothing new,*
> *but it has received a great deal of press*
> *coverage in recent months, and with*
> *that press coverage has come a certain*
> *degree of hype based on the threat's*
> *mystique."*

The Threat of the Lone-Wolf Terrorist Is Exaggerated

Scott Stewart

Scott Stewart was a former agent for the US State Department and is a current analyst for Stratfor Global Intelligence. In the following viewpoint, he maintains that the US government and intelligence community are right to be concerned about the threat of a lone-wolf terrorist. Stewart suggests, however, that such a threat must be neither overstated nor ignored. He traces the history of the lone-wolf terrorist and the spread of the leaderless resistance model, which emerged from the late 1980s as an attempt by white supremacist groups to evade government surveillance. In practice, Stewart notes, lone-wolf terrorism faces a number of formidable challenges; the lone wolf must have the skill, discipline, and resourcefulness to succeed against numerous obstacles.

As you read, consider the following questions:

1. According to Stewart, what former Ku Klux Klan leader published an influential essay in his magazine the *Seditionist* that advocated the leaderless resistance model for white supremacist groups?

2. What military theoretician does the author identify as the first one to promote the concept of the leaderless resistance model to Islamic extremist groups?

3. What did lone-wolf terrorist Roshonara Choudhry do in 2010?

Lone wolf. The mere mention of the phrase invokes a sense of fear and dread. It conjures up images of an unknown, malicious plotter working alone and silently to perpetrate an unpredictable, undetectable and unstoppable act of terror. This one phrase combines the persistent fear of terrorism in modern society with the primal fear of the unknown.

The phrase has been used a lot lately. Anyone who has been paying attention to the American press over the past few weeks has been bombarded with a steady stream of statements regarding lone-wolf militants. While many of these statements, such as those from President Barack Obama, Vice President Joseph Biden and Department of Homeland Security director Janet Napolitano, were made in the days leading up to the 10th anniversary of the 9/11 attacks [referring to the September 11, 2001, terrorist attacks on the United States], they did not stop when the threats surrounding the anniversary proved to be unfounded and the date passed without incident. Indeed, on Sept. 14, the director of the National Counterterrorism Center, Matthew Olsen, told CNN that one of the things that concerned him most was "finding that next lone-wolf terrorist before he strikes."

Now, the focus on lone operatives and small independent cells is well founded. We have seen the jihadist threat devolve from one based primarily on the hierarchical al Qaeda core organization to a threat emanating from a broader array of grassroots actors operating alone or in small groups. Indeed, at present, there is a far greater likelihood of a successful jihadist attack being conducted in the West by a lone-wolf attacker or small cell inspired by al Qaeda than by a member of the al Qaeda core or one of the franchise groups. But the lone-wolf threat can be generated by a broad array of ideologies, not just jihadism. A recent reminder of this was the July 22 attack in Oslo, Norway, conducted by lone wolf Anders [Behring] Breivik.

The lone-wolf threat is nothing new, but it has received a great deal of press coverage in recent months, and with that press coverage has come a certain degree of hype based on the threat's mystique. However, when one looks closely at the history of solitary terrorists, it becomes apparent that there is a significant gap between lone-wolf theory and lone-wolf practice. An examination of this gap is very helpful in placing the lone-wolf threat in the proper context.

The Shift Toward Leaderless Resistance

While the threat of lone wolves conducting terrorist attacks is real, the first step in putting the threat into context is understanding how long it has existed. To say it is nothing new really means that it is an inherent part of human conflict, a way for a weaker entity—even a solitary one—to inflict pain upon and destabilize a much larger entity. Modern lone-wolf terrorism is widely considered to have emerged in the 1800s, when fanatical individuals bent on effecting political change demonstrated that a solitary actor could impact history. Leon Czolgosz, the anarchist who assassinated U.S. president William McKinley in 1901, was one such lone wolf.

The 1970s brought lone-wolf terrorists like Joseph Paul Franklin and Ted Kaczynski, both of whom were able to operate for years without being identified and apprehended. Based on the success of these lone wolves and following the 1988 Fort Smith Sedition Trial, in which the U.S. government's penetration of white hate groups was clearly revealed, some of the leaders of these penetrated groups began to advocate "leaderless resistance" as a way to avoid government pressure. They did not invent the concept, which is really quite old, but they readily embraced it and used their status in the white supremacist movement to advocate it.

In 1989, William Pierce, the leader of a neo-Nazi group called the National Alliance and one of the Fort Smith defendants, published a fictional book under the pseudonym Andrew Macdonald titled *Hunter*, which dealt with the exploits of a fictional lone wolf named Oscar Yeager. Pierce dedicated the book to Joseph Paul Franklin and he clearly intended it to serve as an inspiration and model for lone-wolf operatives. Pierce's earlier book, *The Turner Diaries*, was based on a militant operational theory involving a clandestine organization, and *Hunter* represented a distinct break from that approach.

In 1990, Richard Kelly Hoskins, an influential "Christian Identity" ideologue, published a book titled *Vigilantes of Christendom* in which he introduced the concept of the "Phineas Priest." According to Hoskins, a Phineas Priest is a lone-wolf militant chosen by God and set apart to be God's "agent of vengeance" upon the earth. Phineas Priests also believe their attacks will serve to ignite a wider "racial holy war" that will ultimately lead to the salvation of the white race.

In 1992, another of the Fort Smith defendants, former Ku Klux Klan leader Louis Beam, published an essay in his magazine the *Seditionist* that provided a detailed road map for moving the white hate movement toward the leaderless resistance model. This road map called for lone wolves and small "phantom" cells to engage in violent action to protect themselves from detection.

The Leaderless Resistance Model

In the white supremacist realm, the shift toward leaderless resistance—taken because of the government's success in penetrating and disrupting group operations—was an admission of failure on the part of leaders like Pierce, Hoskins and Beam. It is important to note that in the two decades that have passed since the leaderless resistance model rose to prominence in the white supremacist movement there have been only a handful of successful lone-wolf attacks. The army of lone wolves envisioned by the proponents of leaderless resistance never materialized.

But the leaderless resistance model was advocated not only by the far right. Influenced by their anarchist roots, left-wing extremists also moved in that direction, and movements such as the Earth Liberation Front and the Animal Liberation Front actually adopted operational models that were very similar to the leaderless resistance doctrine prescribed by Beam.

More recently, and for similar reasons, the jihadists have also come to adopt the leaderless resistance theory. Perhaps the first to promote the concept in the jihadist realm was jihadist military theoretician Abu Musab al-Suri. Upon seeing the success the United States and its allies were having against the al Qaeda core and its wider network following 9/11, al-Suri began to promote the concept of individual jihad—leaderless resistance. As if to prove his own point about the dangers of belonging to a group, al-Suri was reportedly captured in November 2005 in Pakistan.

Al-Suri's concept of leaderless resistance was embraced by al Qaeda in the Arabian Peninsula (AQAP), the al Qaeda franchise group in Yemen, in 2009. AQAP called for this type of strategy in both its Arabic-language media and its English-language magazine, *Inspire*, which published long excerpts of al-Suri's material on individual jihad. In 2010, the al Qaeda core also embraced the idea, with U.S.-born spokesman Adam Gadahn echoing AQAP's calls for Muslims to adopt the leaderless resistance model.

The Case of Anders Behring Breivik

On 22 July, Norway was struck by two sequential terrorist attacks. The first was a car bomb that exploded outside a government office in the capital, Oslo. The apparent target, Prime Minister Jens Stoltenberg, was not harmed, but eight people were killed and several others injured. About an hour later, Anders Behring Breivik traveled to the island of Utøya, where the Labour Party (Stoltenberg's political party) was holding a youth camp. Breivik, disguised as a policeman, opened fire on the campers, most of them teenagers, killing sixty-eight before police arrived, when he surrendered peacefully. Breivik, also the suspect in the Oslo bombing, is a 32-year-old Norwegian described as an ultra-right-wing extremist. On the day of the attacks, he posted an Islamophobic, ultranationalist manifesto online, expressing strong support for the eradication of Islam and multiculturalism in order to save Christian Europe. The attacks underscored for law enforcement agencies around the world that domestic political extremists are more likely to perpetrate terrorist attacks than foreign Islamic radicals.

"Islamophobia,"
Global Issues in Context *Online Collection, 2014.*

However, in the jihadist realm, as in the white supremacist realm before it, the shift to leaderless resistance was an admission of weakness rather than a sign of strength. Jihadists recognized that they have been extremely limited in their ability to successfully attack the West, and while jihadist groups welcomed recruits in the past, they are now telling them it is too dangerous because of the steps taken by the United States and its allies to combat the transnational terrorist threat.

Busting the Mystique

Having established that when a group promotes leaderless resistance as an operational model it is a sign of failure rather than strength, let's take a look at how the theory translates into practice.

On its face, as described by strategists such as Beam and al-Suri, the leaderless resistance theory is tactically sound. By operating as lone wolves or small, insulated cells, operatives can increase their operational security and make it more difficult for law enforcement and intelligence agencies to identify them. As seen by examples such as Fort Hood shooter Nidal [Malik] Hasan and Roshonara Choudhry, who stabbed British lawmaker Stephen Timms with a kitchen knife in May 2010, such attacks can create a significant impact with very little cost.

Lone wolves and small cells do indeed present unique challenges, but history has shown that it is very difficult to put the lone-wolf theory into practice. For every Eric Rudolph, Nidal Hasan and Anders [Behring] Breivik there are scores of half-baked lone-wolf wannabes who either botch their operations or are uncovered before they can launch an attack.

It is a rare individual who possesses the requisite combination of will, discipline, adaptability, resourcefulness and technical skill to make the leap from theory to practice and become a successful lone wolf. Immaturity, impatience and incompetence are frequently the bane of failed lone-wolf operators, who also frequently lack a realistic assessment of their capabilities and tend to attempt attacks that are far too complex. When they try to do something spectacular they frequently achieve little or nothing. By definition and operational necessity, lone-wolf operatives do not have the luxury of attending training camps where they can be taught effective terrorist tradecraft. Nasir al-Wuhayshi has recognized this and has urged jihadist lone wolves to focus on simple, easily accomplished attacks that can be conducted with readily available items and that do not require advanced tradecraft to succeed.

The Challenges for the Lone-Wolf Terrorist

It must also be recognized that attacks, even those conducted by lone wolves, do not simply materialize out of a vacuum. Lone-wolf attacks must follow the same planning process as an attack conducted by a small cell or hierarchical group. This means that lone wolves are also vulnerable to detection during their planning and preparation for an attack—even more so, since a lone wolf must conduct each step of the process alone and therefore must expose himself to detection on multiple occasions rather than delegate risky tasks such as surveillance to someone else in order to reduce the risk of detection. A lone wolf must conduct all the preoperational surveillance, acquire all the weapons, assemble and test all the components of the improvised explosive device (if one is to be used) and then deploy everything required for the attack before launching it.

Certainly, there is far more effort in a truck bomb attack than a simple attack with a knife, and the planning process is shorter for the latter, but the lone wolf still must follow and complete all the steps. While this operational model offers security advantages regarding communications and makes it impossible for the authorities to plant an informant in a group, it also increases operational security risks by exposing the lone operator at multiple points of the planning process.

Operating alone also takes more time, does not allow the lone attacker to leverage the skills of others and requires that the lone attacker provide all the necessary resources for the attack. When we consider all the traits required for someone to bridge the gap between lone-wolf theory and practice, from will and discipline to self-sufficiency and tactical ability, there simply are not many people who have both the ability and the intent to conduct such attacks. This is why we have not seen more lone-wolf attacks despite the fact that the theory does offer some tactical advantages and has been around for so long.

The limits of working alone also mean that, for the most part, lone-wolf attacks tend to be smaller and less damaging than attacks conducted by independent cells or hierarchical organizations. Breivik's attack in Norway and Hasan's attack at Fort Hood are rare exceptions and not the rule.

An Exaggerated Threat

When we set aside the mystique of the lone wolf and look at the reality of the phenomenon, we can see that the threat is often far less daunting in fact than in theory. One of the most vocal proponents of the theory in the white supremacist movement in the late 1990s was a young California neo-Nazi named Alex Curtis. After Curtis was arrested in 2000 and convicted of harassing Jewish figures in Southern California, it was said that when he made the jump from "keyboard commando" to conducting operations in the physical world he proved to be more of a "stray mutt" than a lone wolf.

Lone wolves—or stray mutts—do pose a threat, but that threat must be neither overstated nor ignored. Lone attackers are not mythical creatures that come out of nowhere to inflict harm. They follow a process and are vulnerable to detection at certain times during that process. Cutting through the hype is an important step in dispelling the mystique and addressing the problems posed by such individuals in a realistic and practical way.

Periodical and Internet Sources Bibliography

The following articles have been selected to supplement the diverse views presented in this chapter.

| Susan Baller-Shepard | "The Very Real Face of Domestic Terrorism," *Huffington Post*, October 7, 2012. |

Peter Bergen and Andrew Lebovich — "Study Reveals the Many Faces of Terrorism," CNN, September 10, 2011.

Michael Friscolanti — "The Self-Radicalized Terrorist Next Door," *Maclean's*, July 22, 2013.

Greg Myre — "Boston Bombings Point to Growing Threat of Homegrown Terrorism," NPR, April 20, 2013.

Bob Orr — "Who Are Most Likely U.S. Domestic Terrorists?," CBS News, July 25, 2011.

Romesh Ratnesar — "Why Homegrown Terrorism Is Hard to Stop," *Bloomberg Businessweek*, April 15, 2013.

David Sirota — "Right-Wing Terrorism Is Real," *Salon*, January 22, 2013.

Sandhya Somashekhar and Carol D. Leonnig — "'Lone Wolf' Domestic Terrorism Threats Are Hard to Track," *Washington Post*, August 8, 2012.

Tim Sorrick — "Political Violence Prevention: Profiling Domestic Terrorists," *Small Wars Journal*, June 6, 2013.

John Tirman — "Does All Terrorism Come from the Right Wing?," *Huffington Post*, August 11, 2012.

How Might the Threat of Domestic Terrorism Be Averted or Prevented?

Chapter Preface

Racial, ethnic, and religious profiling has a long history in the United States. The practice of regarding particular people as more likely to commit crimes because of their race, ethnic heritage, religion, or national origin can be traced back to the Spanish and English settlers, who put into place draconian and discriminatory security policies against native North American people. Such racial profiling policies were justified by settlers to keep law and order and protect the security of vulnerable settlements in the New World.

For hundreds of years, African Americans have also been the subject of racial profiling in the United States. First brought over as slaves and then oppressed after their emancipation in 1863 by discriminatory Jim Crow laws and a racist political, economic, and cultural power structure, African Americans are still reportedly the victims of racial and ethnic profiling in many parts of the country.

Since the terrorist attacks of September 11, 2001, it has been reported that Muslims also have been the victims of racial, ethnic, and religious profiling by law enforcement, federal intelligence agencies, and even the American public. The horrific attacks on the World Trade Center in New York City and the Pentagon in Washington, DC, were perpetrated by nineteen men affiliated with the Islamic jihadist terrorist group al Qaeda, led by the fanatical leader Osama bin Laden. All nineteen hijackers were from Muslim countries in the Middle East. Nearly three thousand people were killed, making it the deadliest terrorist strike in the United States.

Several months before the 9/11 terrorist attacks, President George W. Bush and the US Justice Department had spoken against the practice of racial and ethnic profiling—except when it came to terrorism. In a 2003 Department of Justice memo, the Bush administration took pains to differentiate between the practice of racial and ethnic profiling in criminal investigations and in terrorist investigations. "Since the terrorist attacks on September 11, 2001, the president has emphasized that federal law enforcement personnel must use every legitimate tool to prevent future attacks, protect our nation's borders, and deter those who would cause devastating harm to our country and its people through the use of biological or chemical weapons, other weapons of mass destruction, suicide hijackings, or any other means," the Department of Justice stated.

"Therefore, the racial profiling guidance recognizes that race and ethnicity may be used in terrorist identification, but only to the extent permitted by the nation's laws and Constitution," the department stated.

There have been widespread concerns over the use of racial, ethnic, and religious profiling against the Muslim community by US law enforcement and intelligence agencies since the attack of September 11, 2001. Investigations by civil liberties groups revealed that these federal agencies have been targeting Muslim communities for years, based on little more than demographic information and stereotypes.

The debate over the use of racial, ethnic, and religious profiling to identify domestic terrorist suspects is one of the subjects examined in the following chapter, which surveys ways to address the threat of domestic terrorism. Other viewpoints in the chapter underscore counterterrorism efforts at the community level and confronting hate speech and intolerance.

"The five factors used to identify potential terrorist perpetrators are plausible. However, to be considered plausible some of the factors had to be placed in the correct context."

Profiling Would Help Identify Potential Domestic Terrorists

Tim Sorrick

Tim Sorrick is an engineer and a contributor to Small Wars Journal. *In the following viewpoint, he asserts that it is essential for the US intelligence community to identify potential domestic terrorists to protect the nation's security. To that end, developing a national standard from which to profile potential terrorists would be invaluable. Sorrick maintains that five factors should be used in any profiling scheme: age, immigration, marital status, group affiliation, and psychological makeup. Utilizing unreliable factors, such as religion, will reinforce stereotypes and hinder the intelligence process. Sorrick argues that profiling could be particularly useful in identifying the lone-wolf terrorist, because these lone perpetrators are less likely to be detected by the public or by intelligence agencies and law enforcement through more traditional means.*

As you read, consider the following questions:

1. According to Sorrick, what is the median age for likely terrorist perpetrators?

2. What percentage of domestic terrorist activity in the United States does the author attribute to lone-wolf attacks from 1999–2009?

3. What percentage of prevented terrorist plots in the United States were because of public tips, according to Sorrick?

The events of September 11th, 2001, a terrorist attack against "soft" targets, caused the U.S. intelligence community to seek and develop efforts to detect terrorist operations and plots as far in advance as possible in order to prevent them from taking place. In light of this it is more important than ever to be able to identify potential terrorists. Dr. Sabina Burton who is writing a book on the profiles of domestic terrorists states, "A domestic terrorist can appear almost normal and is camouflaged by their environment, but the process of becoming a violent extremist is a series of steps that leave footprints we should be able to track." A national standard from which to identify individuals who have left these footprints and are on the path to becoming violent would be invaluable to law enforcement, especially at the local level. Without a set standard each local law enforcement agency interprets who may or may not be a threat and what is worth reporting or investigating differently as they have different experiences and expectations about domestic terrorists and terrorism. Domestic terrorists can be identified prior to committing any terrorist attacks through a profiling system based upon identifying factors that influence committing acts of terrorism.

Factors

The five factors of age, immigration, marital status, group affiliation, and psychological makeup were identified from the previous work of another author as possessing the potential to identify individuals before they conduct an act of domestic terrorism. Religion itself was not considered a reliable gauge of potential terrorism—aspects considered likely were limited in scope to contain the amount bias could affect the outcome.

Using the age factor to determine the likelihood of terrorist action is plausible. For terrorist perpetrators the median age is 23 for a high risk and 28 for some risk. This indicates that terrorism perpetrators from 1999–2009 in the United States have tended to be in the late adolescent to young adult age range. Being in that age range would therefore increase the likelihood of the individual to conduct terrorist actions. "Surviving older terrorists become senior leaders and usually attempt to 'graduate' into politics, thereby seeking greater legitimacy." If no longer focused on conducting terrorist actions it follows that the older terrorists would be less likely to perpetrate terrorist actions. The work by Vaisman-Tzachor [Reuben Vaisman-Tzachor, "Psychological Profiles of Terrorists," *Forensic Examiner*, 2006] was the only source located to place a numerical value on terrorist perpetrator age; all other sources that measured age did so qualitatively. The age factor can be used to assist in helping to identify terrorists but is limited to directly identifying the terrorists who carry out any plans—at best indirectly implicating other terrorists involved through any identifiable associations or links to the perpetrator.

The immigration factor applies to a much narrower group of individuals. People in this group who have committed acts of terrorism inside the U.S. have nearly all had an immigration status that was transitional or illegal such as visa overstay violations or illegal immigration. It is unknown if an individual in this factor would come to America with the ultimate goal of committing acts of terrorism or if their immigration status is the cause or result of economic suffering. Economic suffering is also directly linked with the support for political violence. While limited in scope, the immigration factor is plausible.

The factor of marital status and the likelihood of perpetrating terrorism negatively correlate. A reoccurring trend in terrorism perpetrators was that they possessed fewer social and emotional ties to their communities and did not have families of their own—being unmarried. The more developed and committed relationships the individual is in the less likely they are to be involved in conducting terrorist actions. The marital status factor is specific in scope and is plausible, though still unsupported directly by any of the other referenced materials.

The factor of religious, ethnic, or political affiliation positively correlates the extent of an individual's involvement with any Muslim or Arab entities to the likelihood of their involvement in terrorism. However, of the domestic terrorism cases in the U.S. from 1999–2009 less than one-half had links to al Qaeda and its allied movements. The other groups that must be considered relevant are animal rights & environmental groups, white supremacist groups, and other antigovernment extremists as they are also significant sources of domestic terrorism in America. For example in 1968 none of the identifiable terrorist groups operating in the U.S. were religious. It is a common misperception among the American public that Arabs or Muslims are the only extremists who engage in domestic terrorism and we must ensure this heuristic does not permeate any intelligence process.

Fringe Extremist Groups

It is important to point out that these groups are not mainstream groups like the Catholic Church or the Democratic Party, but are loosely affiliated with some type of major group or ideology, existing on the fringes. Terrorists such as Timothy McVeigh, Terry Nichols, José Padilla, and John Walker Lindh were members of such fringe groups before they conducted any acts of terrorism. These fringe groups are significant because they can provide a sense of purpose and acceptance by other individuals who hold similar views. Being surrounded by individuals of similar viewpoints that provide a "complicit surrounding" can turn people toward the path of extremism. A "complicit surrounding" is an insular group whose distinct characteristics influence the individual on a path toward political violence. The group characteristics influence individuals by isolating members from opinions and beliefs that conflict with the group's standards. As information or beliefs that differ from the standard disappear the group standard becomes the accepted norm—not subject to internal examination, review, or critical thinking. It in effect becomes a heuristic the group accepts as truth. Tracking the membership history of such groups could also assist in identifying "lone wolf" terrorists, or those who are not within the command structure of an established group, but may identify with their cause. Lone wolves represent a significant portion of U.S. domestic terrorist as over 40% of cases from 1999–2009 were planned or conducted by this type of terrorist and their plots reach execution nearly twice as often as terrorist plots conducted by groups. This high rate of execution can be attributed to the fact that lone-wolf attacks are difficult to detect because they involve fewer people. The factor of religious, ethnic, or political affiliation is plausible after it has been adjusted to include all major extremist groups and may provide indicators to prevent lone-wolf attacks.

Psychological makeup can provide an indicator of potential terrorist perpetrators. The closer an individual is to pathological narcissism or the Cluster B of personality disorders the more likely they are to become a terrorist perpetrator. This widely accepted disorder is developed throughout life and can be identified by tracing one's history. Ultimately it manifests in a grandiose sense of self and entitlement which collaborates with the development of strong ideological, nationalistic, and/or religious convictions. A narcissistically organized individual is usually starved emotionally and as a result they pur-

© Nikolay Krutlkov/Cartoonstock.com.

sue social affiliation and approval of their groups. This con-
tributes to the terrorist age factor as young males with this
personality disorder are more vulnerable to recruitment tactics that emphasize their specialness. A young male might be
recruited based on a pitch that a group desperately needs him
and his special skills, even though he has no skills or experience. A narcissistic disorder also increases the likelihood of
perpetrating a terrorist action under the factors of marital status and religious, ethnic, or political affiliation. Narcissistic individuals have difficulty in adult interpersonal relationships
and therefore are less likely to be married or have meaningful
ties to their community. In fringe groups a narcissist's affiliation goes beyond what a normal person would experience
manifesting as stronger bonds and with the social group con-
tributing to the exclusion of alternate views and the acceptance of the group's ideology. The psychological makeup factor is plausible and is the most significant of the five factors.

Context

The five factors used to identify potential terrorist perpetrators are plausible. However to be considered plausible some of the factors had to be placed in the correct context. The factor of religious, ethnic, or political affiliation had to be adjusted to apply to relevant groups, not just Muslim or Arab groups. This was supported by quantitative data on the total number of terrorist plots from 1999–2009. Still this has the potential to change based upon the criteria used to define which data of terrorist actions to include. The goals of all included cases were acts of violence intended to cause casualties or catastrophic damage to critical infrastructure. As such 135 animal rights and environmental group attacks were discarded because they were smaller in scale and did not target critical infrastructure such as dams, bridges, power plants, etc. Being nearly 200% of the attacks counted, small-scale animal and environmental incidents could greatly change the results if included.

The five factors, though plausible, are not the most feasible or the most effective historical method in preventing terrorist attacks. In 80% of the foiled plots, initial clues were identified by law enforcement and from public reporting. In these cases law enforcement would not need to profile any of the individuals involved as the initial clue is sufficient to identify the plan or to begin an investigation. These clues did not involve estimating an individual's potential terror but on more tangible elements such as criminal activities, suspicious documents, suspicious activity, and paramilitary training. If tangible evidence is present it reduces the need for profiling. Because of the reduced need the five factors would likely fall under the remaining 20% of foiled terrorist plots and there is no easy way to determine how many of those may or may not have used or benefited from profiling. There is also no way to definitively answer how many more terrorist operations would be foiled if the five factors were incorporated into a standard, but it can be speculated that the number would increase.

Profiling the Lone-Wolf Terrorist

The area in which profiling could be useful is in identifying lone-wolf terrorist attacks as they are executed nearly twice as often as other attacks. This is under the assumption that lone-wolf attacks are more successful because the clues that alert the general public and law enforcement are less apparent or nonexistent. It would also involve an intelligence agency to track the individual over an extended period of time. An agency that is not concerned with arresting or detaining would be free from the pressures of case-based intelligence, enabling them instead to pursue preemptive intelligence where the profiling may be useful.

In order to prevent domestic terrorist attacks, resources should be allocated into improving existing efforts that have proven to be effective as well as into the development and implication of concepts that improve weak areas of domestic terrorist threat detection such as a profiling system. Of the prevented terrorist plots, 40% were prevented from public tips. Therefore, efforts should be made to improve or maintain relationships with local communities and avoid actions which may alienate them. Future research should include classified data to increase accuracy in measuring effectiveness of other domestic counterterrorism measures. A thorough report detailing domestic terrorism incidents will assist policy makers in correctly allocating counterterrorism resources. A comprehensive national profiling system is plausible but will only be effective in instances where there are insufficient tips to begin an investigation or operation, where it does not harm relationships with the general public—as they are a major source of information for preventing domestic terrorism—and where it includes all relevant data from classified sources.

"*Terrorists come from diverse back-grounds and, as law enforcement officials acknowledge, are aware of profiles and how to avoid them.*"

Profiling Is a Flawed Counterterrorism Policy

Elizabeth Goitein and Faiza Patel

Elizabeth Goitein and Faiza Patel are codirectors of the Liberty and National Security program at the Brennan Center for Justice at the New York University School of Law. In the following viewpoint, they argue that racial, ethnic, and religious profiling are ineffective counterterrorism strategies. Goitein and Patel point out that although the US government realized that racial and ethnic profiling was discriminatory and unproductive, religious profiling has remained a popular strategy due to a belief that Muslim religiosity is a sign of potential terrorism. The authors maintain that singling out Muslims based on adherence to religious dictates is discriminatory and violates America's founding principles of religious freedom. Also, it is a failed counterterrorism strategy because terrorists come from diverse racial, ethnic, religious, and ideological backgrounds, and profiling will only serve to alienate communities that would otherwise cooperate with law enforcement.

As you read, consider the following questions:

1. According to the authors, in what year did the US Justice Department prohibit racial and ethnic profiling?

2. What percentage of recent terrorist plots do the authors contend have been foiled with the help of Muslim communities?

3. According to FBI reports, how many hate crimes against Muslims were reported between 2001 and 2009?

The Senate Judiciary Committee's first hearing on racial profiling since 9/11 [referring to the September 11, 2001, terrorist attacks on the United States] took place today [April 17, 2012], in the shadow of teenager Trayvon Martin's killing and allegations that race played a role in his death and in its investigation. The struggle to eliminate racial bias, not only from policing but also from how Americans view and treat one another, is a long-standing and familiar one. But at today's hearing, there will be a new and unwelcome guest at the table: religious profiling.

Racial profiling absorbed Americans' attention in the late 1990s when empirical studies established what black and Hispanic Americans had long known: Cops often selected drivers or pedestrians to stop and question based on race or ethnicity. The studies also showed that this discrimination didn't help the police. The odds of finding illegal substances were roughly the same for targeted minorities and for whites.

The data led to a widespread societal consensus against racial profiling, as well as state laws and police policies barring the practice. In 2003, the Department of Justice issued guidance prohibiting racial and ethnic profiling by federal law enforcement agencies, which it characterized as "invidious discrimination" undermining our commitment to liberty and justice for all.

Islamophobia and Profiling

In the post-9/11 [referring to the September 11, 2001, terrorist attacks] United States, Islamophobia [discrimination against Muslims] has most notably manifested itself in the form of racial profiling. At airports, people in Muslim garb have been denied access to airplanes by security officials who pegged them as potential terrorists. As recently as January of 2009, a party of nine Muslim passengers (three of whom were young children, eight of whom were born in America) was ordered to leave an AirTran [Airways] flight leaving Orlando, Florida, because two other passengers reported that one of them had made a "suspicious remark." However, Kashif Irfan, one of the passengers told to leave the plane, insisted he and his companions were made to do so because of their appearance. Incidents of physical violence directed at Muslims have also occurred on American soil. In September 2007, a Muslim woman named Zohreh Assemi was robbed, sliced with a box cutter, and brutally beaten by a man who called her a "terrorist" and warned her to "get out of town."

"Islamophobia,"
Global Issues in Context *Online Collection, 2014.*

However, the Justice Department's guidance applies only to race and ethnicity, not religion. It excludes national and border security matters, and it doesn't cover state or local law enforcement. In short, it doesn't address the discrimination that has become a fact of life for many American Muslims.

The Rise of Religious Profiling

Since 9/11, law enforcement officials have targeted Muslims for increased scrutiny without any basis to suspect wrongdoing. The New York City Police Department's (NYPD) years-long operation to map and monitor Muslims' everyday lives, infiltrate mosques to keep tabs on how Muslims worship, and track Muslim student groups at universities from Yale to Brooklyn College is just the most egregious example. The FBI [Federal Bureau of Investigation] has conducted similar mapping programs and, as revealed in court cases in New York and California, sent informants to conduct general surveillance at mosques. At the border, customs officials have asked American Muslims returning home questions such as: "What is your religion?" "What mosque do you attend?" "How often do you pray?" "Why did you convert to Islam?" and "Do you recruit people for Islam?"

Such practices appear linked to a belief that religiosity among Muslims is a sign of potential terrorism. Both the NYPD and the FBI have produced analyses that purport to identify behaviors exhibited by individuals on the path to becoming terrorists. Many of these behaviors—which police are encouraged to look for—are standard religious practices shared by millions of American Muslims, including growing a beard, frequently attending a mosque, and giving up alcohol and cigarettes.

Like racial profiling, religious profiling is "invidious discrimination" that is inimical to America's founding principles. The first settlers and many of our ancestors came here fleeing religious persecution, and the free exercise of religion is the first individual right enshrined in the Constitution. But when police openly use the practice of Islam as a proxy for terrorist tendencies, American Muslims hesitate to pray at mosques and sometimes even try to hide their religious identity.

The Ineffective Strategy

Religious profiling is also ineffective. Terrorists come from diverse backgrounds and, as law enforcement officials acknowledge, are aware of profiles and how to avoid them. As they comprise a miniscule fraction of any given religion or ethnic-ity, it's unlikely that programs focusing on entire communities will be successful in identifying terrorists. For example, there is no evidence that the NYPD's infiltration of mosques uncov-ered any terrorist plots that did not originate with the police themselves. Moreover, as with racial profiling, religious profil-ing alienates those profiled—in this case, American Muslims. This is a step backward for counterterrorism efforts, as the co-operation of Muslim communities has been crucial to foiling some 35 percent of recent terrorist plots.

Religious profiling, like racial profiling, perpetuates nega-tive stereotypes held by the public. In a recent Gallup poll, most Americans held an unfavorable view of Islam. Many state legislatures are considering "anti-Sharia" legislation that would come close to criminalizing the practice of Islam. American Muslims' efforts to build mosques where their fami-lies and communities can gather have encountered protests, lawsuits, and even zoning law changes. Most disturbing, the FBI reports that there were over 1,500 hate crimes against Muslims between 2001 and 2009—the brutal murder of Shaima Alawadi, a mother of five, being only the most recent example.

Our law enforcement agencies have a solemn responsibil-ity to keep us safe. Nevertheless religious profiling, like racial profiling, betrays our values without any benefit to our secu-rity. Instead of relying on stereotypes, law enforcement offi-cials should focus on signs of actual criminal conduct. And they should build strong, trusting relationships with American Muslim communities—relationships that will enable us to more effectively fight our common enemy.

> *"In today's threat environment, preventing terrorist attacks means creating a unified effort across all levels of government, and ensuring that law enforcement officers on the front lines at all levels have everything necessary to do their jobs."*

Empowering Communities and Local Law Enforcement Is Essential to Counterterrorism Efforts

Janet Napolitano

Janet Napolitano is the former US secretary of homeland security. In the following viewpoint, she outlines the evolving terrorist threat to the United States, emphasizing the potential of homegrown terrorists to increase the likelihood of successful terrorist attacks. Napolitano surveys some of the initiatives implemented by the Department of Homeland Security to address the domestic terrorist risk. One of the major strategies of the federal government is to make sure that local law enforcement, first re-

Janet Napolitano, "Nine Years After 9/11: Confronting the Terrorist Threat to the Homeland," Statement before the US Senate Committee on Homeland Security and Governmental Affairs, September 22, 2010. Source: Committee on Homeland Security, US House of Representatives, 2010.

sponders, and other local agencies have the information they need to detect and prevent terrorist activity and the resources they need to formulate effective counterterrorism policies. As to those resources, she lists extensive training for state and local law enforcement and the organization of a series of regional summits to bring together community leaders and state and local law enforcement to exchange ideas and identify best practices.

As you read, consider the following questions:

1. How does Napolitano describe the function and significance of the fusion center?

2. What does Napolitano identify as the familiar slogan developed by the Metropolitan Transportation Authority in New York City with support from the Department of Homeland Security?

3. According to Napolitano, the attempted terrorist attack on Northwest Airlines Flight 253 on December 25, 2009, endangered individuals from how many foreign countries?

Today I would like to highlight the main ways in which the terrorist threat to our country is changing—ways that increasingly challenge law enforcement and the intelligence community. I would also like to highlight some specific—though not exhaustive—ways that the Department of Homeland Security is moving to address this evolving threat.

The Evolving Terrorist Threat to the Homeland

The terrorist threat changes quickly, and we have observed important changes in the threat even since this Committee [on Homeland Security and Governmental Affairs] convened a similar hearing last year [2009]. The threat is evolving in several ways that make it more difficult for law enforcement or the intelligence community to detect and disrupt plots.

One overarching theme of this evolution is the diversification of the terrorist threat on many levels. These include the sources of the threat, the methods that terrorists use, and the targets that they seek to attack.

Sources of the threat. It is clear that the threat of al Qaeda–style terrorism is not limited to the al Qaeda core group, or organizations that have close operational links to al Qaeda. While al Qaeda continues to threaten America directly, it also inspires its affiliates and other groups and individuals who share its violent ideology and seek to attack the United States claiming it is in the name of Islam—a claim that is widely rejected.

Some of these affiliates, like al-Shabaab in Somalia, have not yet attempted to attack the homeland, though al-Shabaab has committed acts of terrorism elsewhere and some al-Shabaab leaders have espoused violent anti-American beliefs. Other al Qaeda affiliates have actually attempted to attack the homeland in recent months. These include Tehrik-e Taliban Pakistan (TTP) and al Qaeda in the Arabian Peninsula (AQAP)—which, until their respective claims of responsibility for the attempted Times Square and Christmas Day terrorist attacks, had only conducted attacks in their regions.

Homegrown terrorists represent a new and changing facet of the terrorist threat. To be clear, by "homegrown," I mean terrorist operatives who are U.S. persons and who were radicalized in the United States and learned terrorist tactics either here or in training camps in places such as the Federally Administered Tribal Areas of Pakistan. Terrorist organizations are increasingly seeking operatives who are familiar with the United States or the West. In their roles as terrorist planners, operational facilitators, and operatives, these individuals improve the terrorist groups' knowledge of Western and American culture and security practices, which can increase the likelihood that an attempted attack could be successful. In recent attacks, we have also seen the influence of violent extremist messages and propaganda spread by U.S.-born, English-speaking individuals operating from abroad, including the U.S-born, Yemen-based Anwar al-Awlaki. Skillfully contrived publications, persuasive messages in idiomatic English, and skillful use of the Internet may be helping to increase the number of homegrown violent extremists.

Diversified tactics. Terrorist tactics continue to evolve and diversify. Recent attempted terrorist attacks have proceeded quickly, with less extensive preoperational planning than previous attempts and with fewer linkages to international terrorist organizations. They have been executed on a smaller scale than the catastrophic attacks of 9/11 [referring to the September 11, 2001 terrorist attacks on the United States].

There is a rising threat from attacks that use improvised explosive devices (IEDs), other explosives, and small arms. This type of attack has been common in hot spots around the world for some time, but we have now experienced such attempted attacks in the United States. Other countries, from Afghanistan to Somalia to Russia, have also experienced attacks where small teams of operatives storm a facility using small arms. Unlike large-scale, coordinated, catastrophic attacks, executing smaller-scale attacks requires less planning and fewer preoperational steps. Accordingly, there are fewer opportunities to detect such an attack before it occurs.

Potential targets. Last, let me address targets. We must recognize that virtually anything is a potential target. Consequently, our thinking needs to be "outside the box" while we simultaneously focus our planning on targets that intelligence forecasts to be most at risk. Many of the targets that terrorists seek to strike are familiar—especially commercial aviation, which continues to be a favored target. Most public places and critical infrastructure face some risk of attack in today's environment. Potential targets include mass transit and passenger rail, which serve thousands of people every day, operate on predictable schedules, and have many access points, all of which are appealing characteristics to terrorists. We also see a threat to the kinds of places that are easily accessible to the public. Among these kinds of targets, hotels were notably attacked during the Mumbai terrorist attacks of 2008. There also continues to be a general risk to our critical infrastructure such as ports and chemical facilities.

The increasing number of terrorism sources, terrorist tactics, and terrorist targets makes it more difficult for law enforcement or the intelligence community to detect and disrupt plots. The threats come from a broader array of groups and regions. It comes from a wider variety of harder-to-detect tactics. And it is aimed at harder-to-secure places than before.

DHS [Department of Homeland Security] is moving swiftly to address the current threat landscape. Through the state and major urban area fusion centers, we have been working closely with state, local, tribal, and territorial (SLTT) law enforcement in our overall efforts to combat terrorism, because in an environment where operatives may not have close links to international terrorist organizations—and where they may, in fact, be based within this country—these levels of law enforcement may be the first to notice something suspicious. We have established programs that facilitate a strong, two-way flow of threat-related information, where SLTT officials communicate possible threat information to federal officials, and vice versa. As discussed earlier, preoperational activity—such as target selection, reconnaissance, and dry runs—may occur over a very short time period, or in open and crowded places. Informing federal authorities of suspicious activities allows this information to be compared with information in other law enforcement and intelligence databases and to be analyzed for trends, increasing the likelihood that an attack can be thwarted. This also allows federal authorities to better inform communities of the threats they face. The nation's fusion centers have been a hub of these efforts, combined with other initiatives DHS has instituted to better partner with SLTT law enforcement. Today I will focus on a few of these actions.

Providing Law Enforcement Personnel with the Information and Resources They Need

Information sharing. In today's threat environment, preventing terrorist attacks means creating a unified effort across all levels of government and ensuring that law enforcement officers on the front lines at all levels have everything necessary to do their jobs.

We are strengthening the networks and relationships necessary to get information where it should be, when it should be there, and in the most useful format. At the heart of this effort are fusion centers, which serve as focal points for information sharing among federal and SLTT law enforcement. Starting with just a handful in 2006, there are 72 fusion centers today. They analyze information and identify trends in order to effectively share timely intelligence with local law enforcement and DHS. In turn, DHS shares this information with others within the intelligence community. By doing this, the department facilitates two-way communication among our federal partners and state and local emergency management and public safety personnel, including the first responders on the ground.

My goal is to make every fusion center a center of analytic excellence that provides useful, actionable information about threats to SLTT law enforcement and first responders. To support this vision, we have deployed experienced DHS intelligence officers to fusion centers across the country. We have provided 64 personnel at last count and are committed to having an officer in each fusion center. We support fusion centers in our grants process and are looking for ways to support them through adding technology and personnel, including the deployment of highly trained experts in critical infrastructure protection. As fusion centers become fully operational, we deploy the Homeland Security Data Network so that fusion center personnel with appropriate federal security clearances have access to classified homeland security threat information.

Strengthening fusion centers is not the only way we are improving the flow and quality of information and getting it to where it needs to be. We are also working closely with the Department of Justice to expand the Suspicious Activity Reporting (SAR) initiative into a national resource for SLTT law enforcement. As I mentioned earlier, today's diffuse threat landscape means that a police officer on the beat, rather than an intelligence analyst in Washington, D.C., may have the best opportunity to detect an attack or attack planning. The SAR initiative creates a standard process for law enforcement in more than two dozen states and cities to identify and report suspicious incidents or behaviors associated with specific threats or terrorism. It makes first responders first preventers, as well. The system allows the information to be shared nationally so that it can be used to identify broader trends. We are working with our partners at DOJ to expand this program to every state to make it as comprehensive and effective as possible. By next month, the system will be implemented in an additional 17 locations in addition to the 12 operational, and will cover nearly 70 percent of the American population. We plan for it to be fully implemented on a national scale by the end of 2011.

Grants and grand guidance. Another important way we push tools and resources from Washington and into local hands is through grants. Currently, state and local governments across America are struggling to pay their bills and fund vital services. As a former two-term governor, I know the hard budgetary choices they are facing. But it is critical to our national security that local communities maintain and continue to strengthen their public safety capabilities. To help ease the burden on state and local governments, we awarded $3.8 billion in grants this past year to states, cities, law enforcement, and first responders, and are helping localities stretch these dollars even further. We have eliminated red tape by streamlining the grant process. We have expanded grants to fund maintenance and sustainability, enabling local jurisdictions to support previous investments, rather than buying new equipment or technology each year. We have also bolstered first responders across the country by making it easier for fire grants to be put to work quickly and to enable fire departments to rehire laid-off firefighters and protect the jobs of veteran firefighters. Keeping experienced first responders on the job is critical to our ability to recognize threats and take action.

Public awareness. As recent events have underscored, each and every person has a role to play in keeping our communities and country safe. For example, take the New York street vendor who tipped off a policeman about the bombing attempt in Times Square, or the group of passengers on Flight 253 who intervened to stop the bombing attempt on Christmas Day.

That is why we have taken an effective public awareness campaign with a familiar slogan—"If You See Something, Say Something"—developed by New York City's Metropolitan Transportation Authority with support from DHS, and are expanding it across the country, throughout various sectors. Over the summer, we launched this campaign in partnership with Amtrak, the general aviation community, and local and regional law enforcement in the National Capital Region and across the Southern states. We are also working with professional and collegiate sports leagues to launch this effort at stadiums across the country this fall.

The goal of the "If You See Something, Say Something" campaign is to raise awareness of potential indicators of terrorism, crime and other threats and emphasize the importance of reporting suspicious activity to law enforcement. We see this as a way both to empower Americans to take part in

Domestic Terrorism in the United States

- There were a total of 207 terrorist attacks in the United States between 2001 and 2011. . . .

- Between 2001 and 2011, we recorded a total of 21 fatal terrorist attacks in the United States.

- The highest proportion of unsuccessful attacks since 1970 occurred in 2011, when four out of nine recorded attacks were unsuccessful. . . .

- The three cities in the United States that experienced the most attacks from 2001 to 2011 were New York City (12), Washington, DC (9) and Los Angeles (8).

- The most common weapons used in terrorist attacks in the United States from 2001 to 2011 were incendiary devices (53% of all weapons used) and explosives (20% of all weapons used).

- For the period from 2001 to 2011, biological weapons were tied with firearms as the third most common weapon used in terrorist attacks (both represented 8% of all weapons used). This unusual result is due to the anthrax attacks in October 2001. . . .

- From 2001 to 2011, the most common targets of terrorists in the United States were businesses (62 attacks), private citizens and property (59 attacks), and government (43 attacks).

"Integrated United States Security Database (IUSSD): Data on the Terrorist Attacks in the United States Homeland, 1970 to 2011," National Consortium for the Study of Terrorism and Responses to Terrorism, December 2012.

our nation's security and to build important relationships between citizens and SLTT law enforcement in order to ensure local authorities have the information they need to stop terrorist attacks.

Empowering Communities and Police to Combat Violence

We also are empowering local jurisdictions and communities to work together to address violent extremism. The potential threat of homegrown violent extremism is very clear. Some two dozen Americans have been arrested on terror charges since 2009. While it is not clear if this represents an actual increase in violent radicalization, versus a rise in the mobilization of previously radicalized individuals, it is nonetheless evident that over the past 12 months, efforts by violent extremist groups and movements to communicate with and recruit individuals within the United States have intensified. And the profiles of Americans who have been arrested on terror charges, or who we know are involved in terrorism overseas, indicate that there is no "typical" profile of a homegrown terrorist. While we work to address violent extremism, we must acknowledge that there is much we do not know about how individuals come to adopt violent extremist beliefs.

All of this was noted in a detailed report by the Bipartisan Policy Center's National Security Preparedness Group cochaired by Lee Hamilton and Tom Kean. It is important to emphasize, though, the actions are currently under way to address the threat of homegrown violent extremism, including our regular consultations with international partners. We know that information-driven, community-oriented approaches led by local police departments in close partnership with community members have been very successful in reducing violence in many American communities. The Homeland Security Advisory Council's (HSAC) Countering Violent Extremism Working Group—comprised of security experts, elected officials, law enforcement leaders, community leaders, and first responders from around the country—has provided DHS with a number of recommendations on how to support local law enforcement and community-based efforts to identify and combat sources of violent extremism.

Based on the HSAC working group's recommendations, and in conjunction with the Major Cities Chiefs Association, the International Association of Chiefs of Police, the Department of Justice, the [National] Counter Terrorism Academy, and the Naval Postgraduate School, we are developing a curriculum for state and local law enforcement focused on community-oriented policing, to enable frontline personnel to identify activities that are indicators of criminal activity and violence. This training will be available through a number of venues, including regional community policing institutes and DHS's Federal Law Enforcement Training Center.

We are producing a series of unclassified case studies that examine recent incidents involving terrorism. These will inform state and local law enforcement personnel, as well as members of communities, about common behaviors and indicators exhibited by the suspects in these cases. DHS is also creating a series of intelligence products for the fusion centers and law enforcement personnel that will discuss tactics, techniques and plans of terrorist organizations, including the recruitment and training of individuals living in the United States.

In addition, DHS is convening a series of regional summits with state and local law enforcement, government, and community leaders this fall to focus on best practices. These summits will allow all participants to provide and receive feedback on successful community-oriented policing and other programs aimed at preventing violence and crime. DHS will gather these case studies and best practices and share them with law enforcement nationwide, employing the widely used platforms that the department has already established.

Finally, DHS continues to work with the Department of Justice to leverage grant programs to support training and technical assistance for SLTT law enforcement. The department is working to incorporate community-oriented policing concepts into our broader preparedness efforts. And at the same time—because these new initiatives and policies are inherently relevant to DHS's local community partnerships—the department is expanding the cultural training and engagement activities performed by the Office for Civil Rights and Civil Liberties. These activities will help both DHS personnel and SLTT law enforcement to better understand, identify, and mitigate threats to American communities.

Community leaders play a vital role in countering violent extremism. Many have helped disrupt plots and have spoken out against violent extremism. They play a central role in addressing this issue, and we are committed to continuing to work closely with them.

Strengthening Specific Sectors

All of what I have described today helps to create a strong foundation for preventing acts of terrorism. But I would also like to talk about some steps we have taken to address terrorist threats to specific economic sectors. These are hardly the only sectors we are focused upon, but there are a few I would like to highlight for the purpose of this testimony.

Commercial aviation. Despite many improvements to aviation security since 9/11 that have made flying very safe, there are still vulnerabilities that need to be addressed. The attempted terrorist attack on Northwest [Airlines] Flight 253, bound to Detroit, on December 25, 2009, illustrated the global nature of the threat to aviation. That incident involved a U.S. plane flying into a U.S. city, but it endangered individuals from at least 17 foreign countries. The alleged attacker, Umar Farouk Abdulmutallab, is a Nigerian citizen educated in the United Kingdom. He received training in terrorist tactics in Yemen, purchased his ticket in Ghana, and flew from Nigeria to Amsterdam before departing for Detroit. And as Canadian officials have pointed out, the plane was over Canadian airspace at the time of the incident.

After this attempted terrorist attack, the U.S. government moved quickly to do more to strengthen security. We took immediate steps to bolster passenger screening, while addressing larger systemic issues on a global scale. I personally traveled to numerous foreign capitals in the aftermath of the attack to work with our allies to ensure our international aviation security efforts were stronger, better coordinated, and redesigned to meet the current threat environment. Since January, we have worked closely with the International Civil Aviation Organization (ICAO), the United Nations body responsible for air transport, on five regional aviation security summits that I have participated in along with elected leaders, security ministers, and airline officials. We have also worked closely with U.S. and international airline and airport trade associations and airline CEOs on a coordinated, international approach to enhancing aviation security.

Next week, at the ICAO General Assembly meeting, we expect the international community to ratify four key elements of global aviation security. These elements are: developing and deploying new security technologies that better detect dangerous materials; strengthening security measures and standards for airport inspections and cargo screening; enhancing information sharing about threats between countries within the international aviation system; and coordinating international technical assistance for the deployment of improved technologies. These reforms represent a historic advancement for the safety and security of air travel.

DHS has coupled these international efforts with significant advances in domestic aviation security. We have deployed additional behavior detection officers, air marshals, and explosives-detection canine teams, among other measures, to airports across the country. Through the president's fiscal year 2011 budget request and the [American] Recovery [and Reinvestment] Act, we accelerated the purchase of 1,000 advanced imaging technology machines for deployment to airports around the country, and are purchasing and deploying more portable explosive detection machines, advanced technology X-ray systems, and bottled liquid scanners. The United States implemented new, enhanced security measures for all air carriers with international flights to the United States that use real-time, threat-based intelligence to better mitigate the evolving terrorist threats. In June, DHS achieved a major aviation security milestone called for in "The 9/11 Commission Report" by assuming responsibility for terrorist watch list screening of all passengers on domestic and international flights on U.S. airlines.

Surface transportation. I would also like to discuss specific actions we have taken to strengthen security for surface transportation, such as passenger rail and mass transit. Many of the steps I have already described are especially important in that environment. We conducted the initial launch of the national "If You See Something, Say Something" campaign at Penn Station in New York, in conjunction with Amtrak. The SAR initiative is also geared toward detecting signs of terrorism in public places like train stations, buses, or railcars. This initiative includes the Amtrak Police Department as a law enforcement partner and allows Amtrak officers to use the upgraded reporting system to refer suspicious activity reports to DHS and the Federal Bureau of Investigation. This is in addition to the intelligence sharing that the Transportation Security Administration (TSA) conducts with Amtrak on an ongoing basis, and the information-sharing work done by the Public Transportation Information Sharing and Analysis Center. The expansion of the SAR initiative will continue to work discretely to secure rail transportation.

There are also a number of operational activities under way focused on surface transportation. We are continuing to augment local antiterrorism efforts by deploying TSA officers at train stations to screen passengers with Amtrak police, and in New York subway stations to work alongside New York and MTA police. TSA special operation teams, known as VIPR [Visible Intermodal Prevention and Response] teams, work with local partners to support several thousand operations every year. We are moving forward on risk-based implementation plans for each of the 20 recommendations (of which DHS has the lead on 19) made in the Surface Transportation Security Assessment, released in April as part of an administration-wide effort to address surface transportation security. We are also in the rule-making process to require background checks and security training for public transit employees, and to require vulnerability assessments and security plans for high-risk public transportation agencies, railroads, and bus operators. All of these will help to address a landscape where the threats to these systems are distinct.

Conclusion

The terrorist threat against the United States continues to evolve in ways that present more complicated and dangerous challenges than we have faced in the past. We cannot guarantee that there will never be another terrorist attack, and we cannot seal our country under a glass dome. But we can do everything in our power to prevent attacks, confront the terrorist threat head-on, and secure our country.

The efforts that I have described today are only a small part of the work that the hundreds of thousands of men and women, at DHS and at law enforcement agencies across the country, do every day to secure our nation. And I want to emphasize that the department is focused on many other threats, as well—in particular, the growing threat to our cyber networks and the threat from chemical, biological, radiological, and nuclear weapons. In everything I have described today—and in everything we do to combat terrorism—DHS is focused on providing those on the front lines with the technology, training, and information they need to do their jobs and keep our country safe.

> "Some experts say the government needs to do a better job with Muslim communities, perhaps their best source of intelligence on terrorist plots, and should avoid heavy-handed tactics and civil liberties abuses that jeopardize trust building."

Better Outreach to the American Muslim Community Should Improve Counterterrorism Efforts

Toni Johnson

Toni Johnson is a journalist and contributor to the website of the Council on Foreign Relations. In the following viewpoint, she asserts that the US intelligence and law enforcement communities are hindered by an "underdeveloped relationship" with the nation's Muslim community and that this interferes with their ability to identify potential domestic terrorists. The United States needs to improve its relationship with these communities, which are an invaluable partner in the fight against homegrown Islamic extremism. Johnson reports that reaching out to these

Toni Johnson, "Threat of Homegrown Islamist Terrorism," Council on Foreign Relations, September 30, 2011. Copyright © 2011 Council on Foreign Relations. Reproduced by permission.

communities is challenging. In many instances, the only govern-
ment agencies that are present and successful in engaging US
Muslim communities are local ones. Johnson concludes that na-
tional agencies need to do a better job in coordinating at the lo-
cal level and formulating a trusting, cooperative relationship
with the community.

As you read, consider the following questions:

1. According to a May 2010 RAND Corporation report,
   how many incidents of "domestic radicalization and recruitment to jihadist terrorism" were reported between
   September 11, 2001, and the end of 2009?

2. According to a September 2010 paper by the Bipartisan
   Policy Center, what seems to be the only common de-
   nominators among the suspects arrested in domestic
   terrorism investigations in the last decade?

3. What does Johnson report as the controversy surrounding Mohamed Osman Mohamud's arrest for domestic
   terrorism?

The number of terror incidents involving Islamic radicals
who are U.S. citizens has seen an uptick in recent years.
U.S. citizens have also been involved in some high-profile international terrorism incidents, such as the 2008 attacks in
Mumbai, India. This has prompted growing questions about
motivations of Islamic radicals in the United States in the decade since the September 11, 2001 [also referred to as 9/11],
terror attacks by al Qaeda that killed nearly three thousand
people. As the list has grown, the question increasingly arises
of how to combat Islamist terrorism at home. U.S. law enforcement intelligence is hampered by an underdeveloped relationship with Muslim communities and the inability to
readily identify potential terrorists—especially since they often
do not appear to need help from international organizations
like al Qaeda to carry out plots.

Islamic Radicalism in the United States

Between September 11, 2001, and the end of 2009, the U.S. government reported forty-six incidents of "domestic radicalization and recruitment to jihadist terrorism" that involved at least 125 people, according to a May 2010 RAND Corporation report. Half the cases involve single individuals, while the rest represent "tiny conspiracies," according to congressional testimony by Brian Michael Jenkins, author of the RAND report.

About one-quarter of the plots identified have links to major international jihadist groups like al Qaeda, according to the RAND report. But a March 2010 Bipartisan Policy Center paper points out an increasing number of Americans are playing high-level operational roles in al Qaeda and aligned groups, as well as a larger number of Americans who are attaching themselves to these groups.

There had been an average of six cases per year since 2001, but that rose to thirteen in 2009, a worrisome sign to some experts. Still, analysts caution against assuming any large-scale radicalization of the U.S. Muslim population. Cases of Muslims involved in domestic terror plots represent a very small minority of the entire U.S. Muslim community, which ranges somewhere between less than 2 million and upwards of 7 million. (U.S. law forbids mandatory questions about religion on the U.S. census, and polling and other estimates have produced a wide range in population numbers.)

"Given the fact that we're dealing with such a miniscule minority of, in this case, the Muslim population, it's extremely difficult to craft national policies that affect the tiny minority, or as we would say, statistically detailed distribution," said Richard Falkenrath, a CFR [Council on Foreign Relations] adjunct senior fellow for counterterrorism and former New York City deputy commissioner for counterterrorism.

Sources of Radicalization

As of January 2010, all but two people arrested in the last decade for domestic terror connected to radical Islam have been male. Otherwise, at least three recent think tank reports have concluded that suspects follow no definitive ethnic or socioeconomic pattern, being both immigrant and native born, and ranging in age from 18 to 70.

"The only common denominator appears to be a newfound hatred for their native or adopted country, a degree of dangerous malleability, and a religious fervor justifying or legitimizing violence that impels these very impressionable and perhaps easily influenced individuals toward potentially lethal acts of violence," argues a September 2010 paper by the Bipartisan Policy Center.

Counterterrorism experts point to online social media sites and charismatic English-speaking preachers, such Anwar al-Awlaki, as a boon for terrorist groups looking to spread their ideology in the United States. The U.S. prison system remains another concern for jihadist recruiting. In January 2010, the Senate Committee on Foreign Relations issued a report on al Qaeda, which found that as many as three dozen U.S. exconvicts thought to have become radicalized in prison may have attended terrorist training camps in Yemen. In 2005, law enforcement officials foiled a plot to attack numerous sites in California by three Muslim men linked to Jam'iyyat Ul-Islam Is-Saheeh, a militant, prison-based Muslim group started in 1997. A March 2010 FBI [Federal Bureau of Investigation] bulletin on radicalization in prison says more study is needed. "Authorities must temper their responses with the understanding that religious conversion differs from radicalization," the report says.

Major Terror Cases

Nearly all of the high-profile domestic terror incidents have resulted in convictions in U.S. federal courts. Here are profiles of major cases:

Domestic Terror

José Padilla. A U.S. citizen on a flight from Pakistan, Padilla was detained in Chicago in 2002 and accused of participating in an al Qaeda plot to detonate a "dirty bomb" on U.S. soil. Padilla, who converted to Islam while in jail, was labeled an "enemy combatant," held in a military prison, and denied access to civilian courts for over three years. In late 2005, as the Supreme Court was weighing the constitutionality of Padilla's detention, he was added to a federal criminal case of two other men accused of supplying money, supplies, and recruits for a North American support cell of Islamic extremists, unrelated to the alleged dirty bomb plot. Padilla was sentenced in 2008 to seventeen years in prison.

Detroit Sleeper Cell. Six days after September 11, 2001, police raided an apartment in Detroit, found video footage of tourist sites like Disneyland and drawings that authorities alleged depicted a U.S. air base in Turkey and a military hospital in Jordan. Four legal immigrants, three from Morocco and one from Algeria, were accused of collecting intelligence for terrorist attacks. Three of the men were subsequently convicted, but the fourth was acquitted. The Justice Department later removed the lead prosecutor from the case, saying he knowingly withheld information that could have proved the group's innocence, which later led to reversal of the convictions.

Faisal Shahzad. A naturalized U.S. citizen from Pakistan, Shahzad attempted to bomb New York's Times Square with a parked car full of explosives in May 2010. Shahzad was inspired by Pakistani militants and told authorities he was a "fan and follower" of radical cleric Anwar al-Awlaki, but appears to have planned the bombing alone. He pled guilty and was sentenced to life in prison without the possibility of parole.

Nidal [Malik] Hasan. Virginia-born Muslim and career military psychiatrist Hasan shot and killed thirteen people and wounded nearly thirty in November 2009 at the Fort Hood army base where he worked. Hasan followed Anwar al-Awlaki's lectures and sent twenty-one emails to him asking what Islamic law said about Muslim-American soldiers killing their colleagues. Awlaki responded twice. Hasan frequently argued that it was immoral for Muslim-American soldiers to fight against fellow Muslims in Iraq and Afghanistan, and found out he was being deployed shortly before his rampage. He will be tried in military court and an investigating officer has recommended capital punishment.

Lackawanna Six. Nearly a year after September 11, six Yemeni-American childhood friends from a Buffalo, NY, suburb were arrested in what was a "showpiece for the Bush administration's war on terror," and one of the first examples of preemptive justice on terrorism. They attended an al Qaeda training camp in Kandahar in the spring of 2001, which some in the group claim was motivated by curiosity. All six pled guilty to providing material support for a terrorist organization and were sentenced to seven to nine years in prison. Some have been released, and three will be granted aliases by the U.S. government upon their release for testifying against al Qaeda.

Fort Dix Plot. Six foreign-born Muslims—including four ethnic Albanians from Macedonia and Kosovo who illegally immigrated, a Palestinian from Jordan turned U.S. citizen, and a legal Turkish immigrant—were arrested in 2007 for a plot targeting the Fort Dix army base in New Jersey. The arrests were made after a store clerk turned in a video showing them shooting guns and calling for jihad. The group had no apparent connection with any international terror organizations. Five of the six received life prison sentences from a federal court in late 2008.

The Portland Seven. This diverse group of American Muslims in Portland, OR, was charged with attempting to join al Qaeda and levy war against the United States in a 2002 and

2003 fifteen-count federal indictment aided by the [USA] PATRIOT Act. One fugitive of the group joined al Qaeda and was killed by Pakistani forces in Afghanistan. The remaining six are serving, or have served, prison time.

Mohamed Osman Mohamud. Somali-born, naturalized U.S. citizen Mohamud penned several articles for the online magazine *Jihad Recollections* in 2009, and U.S. authorities allege he attempted to connect with terrorists in Pakistan. In November 2010, police arrested Mohamud in Portland, OR, for trying to detonate what he believed to be a car bomb during a Christmas-tree lighting ceremony. The bomb was actually a fake planted by the FBI, and some question whether the sting operation represented entrapment.

Terror Abroad

Anwar al-Awlaki. New Mexico–born Anwar al-Awlaki was a radical Muslim cleric accused of recruiting for al Qaeda who increasingly advocated violent jihad. Sometimes called the Osama bin Laden of the Internet, Awlaki corresponded primarily through cyberspace with Fort Hood shooter Nidal Hasan, a Minnesota group that recruited for al-Shabaab, and three of the September 11 hijackers. His lectures were also mentioned by one of the men convicted in the Fort Dix plot, as well as would-be Times Square bomber Faisal Shahzad. In April 2010, the [Barack] Obama administration authorized a targeted killing of Awlaki in Yemen. His father acquired two groups of human rights lawyers to challenge Awlaki's inclusion on a list of people to be killed without trial, but the administration's order was upheld by a federal judge in December 2010. Awlaki was reported killed in Yemen (CBS) on September 30, 2011, by a U.S. air strike, which also killed U.S.-born Samir Khan, editor of an English-language al Qaeda web magazine. The deaths have raised fresh concerns about constitutionality of such operations.

John Walker Lindh. A native Californian, Lindh converted at a local mosque before traveling to Yemen, Pakistan, and Afghanistan to join the Taliban, and was captured in November 2001 as the U.S. military invaded Afghanistan. Due to a plea bargain, Lindh was sentenced to twenty years in prison by a federal court on the condition that he drop claims that he had been mistreated or tortured and that he not speak publicly about the conditions of his sentence.

David Headley. A native of Washington, DC, Headley helped Pakistan-based group Lashkar-e-Taiba identify targets for the 2008 terrorist attacks in Mumbai. Headley was also plotting to attack the Copenhagen offices of the newspaper that published cartoons depicting the prophet Muhammad. After September 11, the Drug Enforcement Administration employed Headley as an informant in Pakistan, despite repeated warnings that he might be a terrorist. Headley pled guilty in 2010 in a U.S. federal court and faces life in prison.

Pakistan Five. Five U.S. citizens who reached out to extremists through YouTube were arrested in Pakistan on their way to fight against U.S. troops in Afghanistan with a jihadist group. The young men of Pakistani, Egyptian, Ethiopian, and Eritrean descent—who attended the same northern Virginia mosque—maintain they traveled for a wedding and to help Muslims displaced by the war in Afghanistan. Pakistani courts sentenced them to ten years in prison.

Somalia Plot. Fourteen Somali-Americans were charged in August 2010 with providing material support and recruits for al-Shabaab, an Islamic militant organization fighting an insurgency in Somalia. Of the group, most were in Somalia at the time of the indictment.

Shirwa Ahmed. In October 2008, Shirwa Ahmed, a Somalia-born U.S. citizen, drove a car full of explosives into a government compound in northern Somalia, killing himself and more than twenty people. Speaking at the Council on

Foreign Relations in February 2009, FBI director Robert S. Mueller said Ahmed was radicalized in his Minnesota hometown of Minneapolis.

Policy Implications

An October 2010 report from the Washington, DC–based American Security Project suggests U.S. policy find strategies that address the "deep-seated perceptions and attitudes" among the Muslim and non-Muslim population that help "fuel the alienation cycle that has helped to make a small but increasing number of Americans more susceptible to extremist ideology."

Some experts say the government needs to do a better job with Muslim communities, perhaps their best source of intelligence on terrorist plots, and should avoid heavy-handed tactics and civil liberties abuses that jeopardize trust building. For example, following the 9/11 terrorist attacks, the FBI began routinely interviewing Arab and Muslim men in the country, which garnered criticism from civil liberties advocates that it unfairly targeted entire communities.

But engaging Muslim communities presents challenges. "The U.S. government runs major national programs, but it's not present in a serious, sustained way in all the communities of interest," says CFR's Falkenrath. "The only government agencies that really are [present] are the local agencies: health departments, education departments, police departments, fire departments. As a practical matter, if you really wanted to do something in this (what is called counter-radicalization), you'd need to find a way to incorporate the government agencies at the local level into such an effort."

Nadia Roumani, director of the American Muslim Civic Leadership Institute, also stresses the importance of coordinating among agencies. "Oftentimes, especially on this issue, there will be one strategy that's been taken by local law enforcement and a different strategy taken by the FBI and a different strategy taken by [the Department of Homeland Security]," she noted in a July 2010 panel discussion. "And then the community's confused [on] who to engage and how these are all connecting." Law experts Tara Lai Quinlan and Deborah Ramirez suggest developing a "nationally coordinated law enforcement–community partnership infrastructure" similar to what is being done to combat radicalism in the United Kingdom.

> *"Confront hate groups, hate speech and prejudice in all its forms. Do it daily, make it socially unacceptable."*

Confronting Prejudice and Hate Speech Is Key to Addressing the Domestic Terrorism Threat

Kenneth Robinson

Kenneth Robinson is a journalist, an expert in security and international terrorism, and an executive at a global security firm. In the following viewpoint, he explores the growing threat posed to US national security from violent extremists motivated by hate and bigotry. Robinson urges people to confront hate speech, hate groups, and all forms of prejudice, especially on the radio, on television, and in print media. If such hate is made socially unacceptable, and the ratings of media outlets decrease, the hate media will slowly disappear. Robinson concludes that the US government must recognize the goals of powerful hate groups and address the threat with all needed resources.

Kenneth Robinson, "Hate: The Elephant in the Room," *Huffington Post*, April 24, 2013. Copyright © 2013 Kenneth Robinson. Reproduced by permission.

As you read, consider the following questions:

1. According to the Southern Poverty Law Center, by how much has the number of hate groups in the United States increased since 2000?

2. How much has the number of "Patriot" groups, including militias, increased since President Barack Obama was elected in 2008, according to the Southern Poverty Law Center?

3. How many domestic terrorist and international jihadist groups does the author estimate might attract extremist individuals in the United States?

"It is important that those engaged in terrorism realize that our determination to defend our values and our way of life is greater than their determination to cause death and destruction to innocent people in a desire to impose extremism on the world" [former prime minister of the United Kingdom Tony Blair].

The cruel act of terrorism that targeted innocent spectators and marathon runners in Boston on April 15th 2013 has called out the "Elephant in the room." It raises the question of how a democracy such as ours should confront the perpetrators of terrorism, whether foreign, or domestic.

What Is Terrorism?

First, I assert that terrorism is not a race or ethnic group, it is a tactic to instill fear in the hearts of free people everywhere. An attack on any of us should be treated as an attack on all of us. Our actions and reactions will determine who changes our way of life.

If we are to confront acts of terrorism, we must first understand their polygon of power. From my professional experience—the most credible source of choice is the Southern Poverty Law Center.

"Since 2000, the number of hate groups [in the United States] has increased by 67 percent. This surge has been fueled by anger and fear over the nation's ailing economy, an influx of non-white immigrants, and the diminishing white majority, as symbolized by the election of the nation's first African-American president.

These factors also are feeding a powerful resurgence of the antigovernment 'Patriot' movement, which in the 1990s led to a string of domestic terrorist plots, including the Oklahoma City bombing. The number of 'Patriot' groups, including armed militias, has grown 813 percent since [President] Obama was elected—from 149 in 2008, to 1,360 in 2012."

We must recognize that this exponential growth is also fueled by the lack of quality of the reporting from the national news media, the legitimacy (or lack thereof) of the pundits they book as guests. Most distressing is the massive growth of "Hate Radio" and the unhelpful rhetoric espoused by a vocal minority of ideologically driven political figures to propel their "wedge issues" into the public debate in order to "legitimize false propaganda about immigrants and other minorities and spread the kind of paranoid conspiracy theories on which militia groups thrive."

How Domestic Terrorism Thrives

The perpetrators of terror all have a similar DNA that drives their polygon of power. It begins with the ACCEPTANCE of their ideology by a self-perceived disenfranchised group. They then seek out and spot those disenfranchised and hopeless for RECRUITMENT (assessment, selection, and training).

These recruits are then pushed into a LOOSELY DISTRIBUTED NETWORK of like-minded domestic terrorists/ international jihadists (financed for global reach), pick a name, pick a country—there is about 60 different active organizations.

Oftentimes these groups are leaderless, making it extremely hard to detect, deter, or prevent a hostile act. "Those carrying out destructive acts operate as 'lone wolves' and small cells, with little or no connection to formal organizations. Ultimately, leaderless resistance has become the most common tactical approach of political terrorists in the West and elsewhere."

They conduct ASYMMETRICAL operations like September 11th [referring to the September 11, 2001, terrorist attacks on the United States] or the April 15th bombing [at the Boston Marathon in 2013], which gives their movement its prestige. This prestige has great appeal to an angry, DISENFRANCHISED radical left- or right-wing fringe group.

This nets them more RESOURCES. This VALIDATION of the ideology then PERPETUATES itself like a self-licking ice cream cone.

Ok, so what's the answer?

- First and foremost, recognition of the threat group, and their goals!

- The U.S. must understand that the HATE & EXTREMIST NETWORK is the ENGINE powering the terrorist grid.

- The challenges ahead are GENERATIONAL.

- This 21st-century threat is in a dangerous growth stage (like Bolshevism in 1905 and National Socialism in 1920).

- Perception of success is critical, it gains adherents, and undermines regional governments and the West's political will to confront and fight it.

- Rules don't apply. Terrorists hide within the population, and they use people as their "precision-guided weapons."

- They stress asymmetric effects, and they refuse to mass.

- They seek to unite regional groups by providing their ideology and resources of recruits, money, weapons, training, and transportation.

The president of the United States has promised that ALL SOURCES OF NATIONAL POWER will be harnessed, internationally or domestically. Not just law enforcement & military power, but political, intelligence, logistical, financial, etc.

As our state and federal government pursues the perpetrators of the April 15th bombing, there is something every citizen can do. It can be accomplished at the dinner table, in your school, and on all social media. Confront hate groups, hate speech and prejudice in all its forms. Do it daily, make it socially unacceptable.

All reasonable viewers and readers should abandon television, radio, and print media that glorifies, or perpetuates, wedge issue rhetoric. The people do have a voice, if you use it.

If we stop watching and listening to them, the corporate interest will outweigh the ratings bait of wedge politics and their political interest.

Only then will meaningful change begin to take form.
Act!

Periodical and Internet Sources Bibliography

The following articles have been selected to supplement the diverse views presented in this chapter.

Trevor Aaronson	"The Informants," *Mother Jones*, September–October, 2011.
Matt Apuzzo	"U.S. to Expand Rules Limiting Use of Profiling by Federal Agents," *New York Times*, January 15, 2014.
Petra Bartosiewicz	"A Permanent War on Terror," *Los Angeles Times*, December 7, 2012.
Petra Bartosiewicz	"To Catch a Terrorist," *Harper's*, August 2011.
Froma Harrop	"Stop the Hysteria over NSA Surveillance," Creators.com, August 6, 2013.
Michael Hirsh	"Stopping Terrorism at the Source," *National Journal*, May 2, 2013.
Brad Knickerbocker	"ACLU: FBI Guilty of 'Industrial Scale' Racial Profiling," *Christian Science Monitor*, October 21, 2011.
Cameron McWhirter, Tamer El-Ghobashy, and David Román	"Authorities Hone Fight Against Terrorism," *Wall Street Journal*, April 17, 2013.
William Saletan	"Stop Freaking Out About the NSA," *Slate*, June 6, 2013.
Al Sharpton	"Profiling Helps the Terrorists," *Huffington Post*, April 24, 2013.
Jessica Stern	"Can Google Make Non-Violence Cool?" *Defining Ideas*, August 25, 2011.
Matthew Waxman	"Policing Terrorism," *Defining Ideas*, May 4, 2012.

OPPOSING
VIEWPOINTS®
SERIES

CHAPTER 4

How Should Domestic Terrorism Be Treated?

Chapter Preface

On March 13, 1963, Ernesto Miranda was arrested in Phoenix, Arizona, as a suspect in the kidnap and rape of a seventeen-year-old girl. An ex-con with a long criminal history, he was identified as the main suspect when his car matched the description of the one used in the crime. After two hours of interrogation, Miranda admitted his role in the attack and wrote a ten-page confession. The rape victim also provided a positive voice identification. Everything seemed to be in order and ready for trial—except that Miranda had never been informed of his right to remain silent or his right to be questioned with an attorney present.

During his interrogation, Miranda was informed of some of his rights. This was clear because at the top of each page of his ten-page confession, a printed certification attested to the fact that "this statement has been made voluntarily and of my own free will, with no threats, coercion, or promises of immunity and with full knowledge of my legal rights, understanding any statement I make can and will be used against me." Because that was clearly printed at the top of each piece of paper, it was assumed that Miranda saw and understood those rights. It was his right to counsel that was violated.

Miranda was assigned a lawyer, Alvin Moore, to help with his defense. Moore asked that the confession be thrown out of court because it was obtained illegally. His objection was overruled. Miranda was convicted of kidnapping and rape and sentenced to twenty to thirty years in prison.

Moore appealed the conviction on the basis of Miranda's illegally obtained confession. The Arizona Supreme Court upheld the charges. Moore appealed to the US Supreme Court, which agreed to hear the case, *Miranda v. Arizona*, in late 1965. The court ruled that Miranda's confession was not admissible in court because of the coercive nature of the interrogation and because the suspect was not made aware of his rights under the US Constitution. Therefore, Miranda's conviction was overturned.

In his opinion, Chief Justice Earl Warren underscored the need for suspects to be fully apprised of their rights under the law. As a result of the decision, police departments all over the country incorporated a full reading of a suspect's rights, known as a Miranda warning, into their arrest procedures. In fact, the US Supreme Court has observed that it "has become embedded in routine police practice to the point where the warnings have become part of our national culture." Throughout the decades since the Miranda warning was established, the court has recognized only one exception to it, known as the "public safety" exception. In 1984 the court found that if there was a legitimate and pressing worry for the safety of police or the public, the police do not have to read the Miranda warning before interrogating the suspect and neutralizing the immediate threat.

The flexibility allowed by the public safety exception is praised by national, state, and local law enforcement, who find it valuable in the investigation of domestic terrorism. Civil libertarians, however, are concerned that it will lead to civil rights violations, including the involuntary confessions of suspects and questioning outside the narrow subjects related to pressing threats to public safety.

The debate over the public safety exception to Miranda warnings and its relationship to domestic terrorism investigations is one of the subjects explored in the following chapter, which considers the various ways domestic terrorism should be treated. Other viewpoints in the chapter examine whether military tribunals or civilian courts are the right forum to try domestic terrorism, the double standard applied to some domestic terrorist suspects, and the prospect of stripping terrorist suspects of their US citizenship.

> *"No matter how unsympathetic accused terrorists are, the precedents the government sets for them matter outside the easy context of questioning them."*

Why Should I Care That No One's Reading Dzhokhar Tsarnaev His Miranda Rights?

Emily Bazelon

Emily Bazelon is a journalist, an author, a senior editor at Slate, *and the Truman Capote Fellow at Yale Law School. In the following viewpoint, she maintains that all Americans should be concerned by the US Justice Department's attempts to significantly expand the public safety exception, which allows law enforcement to interrogate suspects before reading them their Miranda rights if officers believe there is a pressing concern for public safety. Bazelon argues that broadening the public safety exception sets a dangerous precedent for future domestic terrorist investigations. Although it may satisfy Americans who do not want the US government to go soft on terrorist suspects, she predicts that it may lead to police railroading suspects and eliciting false confessions.*

As you read, consider the following questions:

1. According to Bazelon, what 1984 Supreme Court case carved out the public safety exception to the reading of Miranda rights?

2. When does Bazelon say the US Justice Department sent a memo to the FBI to broadly expand the public safety exception?

3. When was that Justice Department memo published by the *New York Times?*

Dzhokhar Tsarnaev [the surviving suspect in the 2013 Boston Marathon bombing] will not hear his Miranda rights before the FBI [Federal Bureau of Investigation] questions him Friday night [April 19, 2013]. He will have to remember on his own that he has a right to a lawyer, and that anything he says can be used against him in court, because the government won't tell him. This is an extension of a rule the Justice Department wrote for the FBI—without the oversight of any court—called the "public safety exception."

There is one specific circumstance in which it makes sense to hold off on *Miranda*. It's exactly what the name of the exception suggests. The police can interrogate a suspect without offering him the benefit of *Miranda* if he could have information that's of urgent concern for public safety. That may or may not be the case with Tsarnaev. The problem is that Attorney General Eric Holder has stretched the law beyond that scenario. And that should trouble anyone who worries about the police railroading suspects, which can end in false confessions. No matter how unsympathetic accused terrorists are, the precedents the government sets for them matter outside the easy context of questioning them. When the law gets bent out of shape for Dzhokhar Tsarnaev, it's easier to bend out of shape for the rest of us.

The Legal History

Here's the legal history. In the 1984 case *New York v. Quarles*, the Supreme Court carved out the public safety exception for a man suspected of rape. The victim said her assailant had a gun, and he was wearing an empty holster. So the police asked him where the gun was before reading him his Miranda rights. That exception was allowable, the court said, because of the immediate threat that the gun posed.

Fine. Good, even—that gun could have put other people in danger. Things start to get murkier in 2002, after the FBI bobbled the interrogation of Zacarias Moussaoui, the 20th 9/11 [referring to the September 11, 2001, terrorist attacks on the United States] hijacker—the one who didn't get on the plane—former FBI special agent Coleen Rowley wrote a memo pleading that "if prevention rather than prosecution is to be our new main goal, (an objective I totally agree with), we need more guidance on when we can apply the *Quarles* 'public safety' exception to *Miranda*'s 5th Amendment requirements." For a while, nothing much happened.

Then the Christmas Day bomber, Umar Farouk Abdulmutallab, was apprehended in December 2009, before he could blow up a plane bound for Detroit. The FBI invoked the public safety exception and interrogated. When the agents stopped questioning Abdulmutallab after 50 minutes and Mirandized him—after getting what they said was valuable information—Abdulmutallab asked for a lawyer and stopped talking. Republicans in Congress denounced the [Barack] Obama administration for going soft.

Next came Faisal Shahzad, caught for attempting to bomb Times Square in May 2010. He was interrogated without Miranda warnings via the public safety exception, and again, the FBI said it got useful information. This time, when the suspect was read his rights, he kept talking.

Critics Speak

But that didn't stop Sen. John McCain and then Sen. Christopher Bond from railing against *Miranda*. "We've got to be far less interested in protecting the privacy rights of these terrorists than in collecting information that may lead us to details of broader schemes to carry out attacks in the United States," Bond said. "When we detain terrorism suspects, our top priority should be finding out what intelligence they have that could prevent future attacks and save American lives," McCain said. "Our priority should not be telling them they have a right to remain silent."

Holder started talking about a bill to broadly expand the exception to *Miranda* a few months later. Nothing came of that idea, but in October of 2010, Holder's Justice Department took it upon itself to widen the exception to *Miranda* beyond the Supreme Court's 1984 ruling. "Agents should ask any and all questions that are reasonably prompted by an immediate concern for the safety of the public or the arresting agents," stated a DoJ [Department of Justice] memo to the FBI that wasn't disclosed at the time. Again, fine and good. But the memo continues, "there may be exceptional cases in which, although all relevant public safety questions have been asked, agents nonetheless conclude that continued unwarned interrogation is necessary to collect valuable and timely intelligence not related to any immediate threat, and that the government's interest in obtaining this intelligence outweighs the disadvantages of proceeding with unwarned interrogation."

A Violation of Rights

Who gets to make this determination? The FBI, in consultation with DoJ, if possible. In other words, the police and the prosecutors, with no one to check their power.

The *New York Times* published the Justice Department's memo in March 2011. The Supreme Court has yet to consider this hole the Obama administration has torn in *Miranda*. In fact, no court has, as far as I can tell.

And so the FBI will surely ask 19-year-old Tsarnaev anything it sees fit. Not just what law enforcement needs to know to prevent a terrorist threat and keep the public safe but anything else it deemed related to "valuable and timely intelligence." Couldn't that be just about anything about Tsarnaev's life, or his family, given that his alleged accomplice was his older brother (killed in a shootout with police)? There won't be a public uproar. Whatever the FBI learns will be secret: We won't know how far the interrogation went. And besides, no one is crying over the rights of the young man who is accused of killing innocent people, helping his brother set off bombs that were loaded to maim, and terrorizing Boston Thursday night and Friday. But the next time you read about an abusive interrogation, or a wrongful conviction that resulted from a false confession, think about why we have Miranda [rights] in the first place. It's to stop law enforcement authorities from committing abuses. Because when they can make their own rules, sometime, somewhere, they inevitably will.

> "The difference between criminals and terrorists is that a failure to get a confession from a criminal leads to a lost conviction, but a failure to extract intelligence from a terrorist can mean the deaths of hundreds or even thousands."

Domestic Terrorism Suspects Should Be Interrogated Before Being Read Their Miranda Rights

Daniel Greenfield

Daniel Greenfield is an author, a journalist, and the Shillman Journalism Fellow at the Freedom Center. In the following viewpoint, he traces the history of Miranda rights in the United States. He says in situations where law enforcement believes there may be imminent terrorist attacks, they should focus on interrogating the suspect and learning any information they can to prevent terrorist activities—the reading of Miranda rights interferes with that process and may stop the flow of essential information. He further maintains that the US Justice Department should be more concerned with protecting the country from ter-

rorist attacks and less about the rights of domestic and foreign terrorists. He suggests that the premature Mirandizing of terrorists is part of a disturbing pattern from the Barack Obama administration, accusing it of dismantling necessary policies that have succeeded in preventing large-scale attacks on the United States.

As you read, consider the following questions:

1. According to Greenfield, in what year was Lois Ann Jameson attacked?

2. Who was the federal judge who barged into Dzhokhar Tsarnaev's hospital room to read the terrorist suspect his Miranda rights?

3. What terrorist suspect does the author identify as Osama bin Laden's son-in-law and spokesman for al Qaeda?

The last showing of *The Longest Day* ended at the Paramount Theater before midnight. After the lights had dimmed and the patrons filed out, their minds still filled with the sights and sounds of soldiers fighting and dying at Normandy, the eighteen-year-old girl who had stood behind the concessions counter handing them popcorn and sodas went home.

A Horrific Crime

It was late at night when she began walking home from the bus stop, but crime rates in Phoenix, Arizona, were only beginning the upward rise that would take hold in the seventies.

In 1963, the year that Lois Ann Jameson was walking home, there had been 222 rapes. Ten years later, that number would stand at 637. Today there are over 2,000 rapes a year in Phoenix; ten times as many. But one of those rapes would be hers. And it would lead to a new standard of protection for murderers and rapists.

Ernesto Miranda wasn't famous yet. The days when he would be selling autographed Miranda warning cards were still ahead of him. For now he was only another son of Mexican immigrants, a tattooed felon working temporary jobs and a rapist on the prowl.

Miranda abducted the girl, drove her out to the desert and raped her. He was arrested, questioned and confessed to the crime. The rest should have been straightforward except that no one had told him that he was entitled to a lawyer. The head of the Phoenix office of the ACLU [American Civil Liberties Union] stepped in and the Miranda warning was born.

The Origins of Miranda Rights

Miranda v. Arizona was part of a string of decisions by the Warren Court [the Supreme Court under Chief Justice Earl Warren] that had begun the year of Lois Ann Jameson's rape. The decisions invented rights which not only obligated taxpayers to provide accused criminals with lawyers, but also made it impossible to question a suspect without his lawyer.

In the case of Lois Ann's rapist, Justice Earl Warren, who proved to be a bigger threat to the Constitution than King George III, went beyond inventing the right to a government lawyer, to invent the rapist's right to be told of a right to a government lawyer.

Warren inverted the Fifth Amendment to claim that the confession of a criminal who had not been told that he did not have to incriminate himself was a violation of the ban on self-incrimination. And he held that it should be assumed that all criminals did not know that they did not have to confess.

The Boston Marathon Bombing

Fifty years after a concession stand girl was raped by a career criminal in the desert, terrorist bombs went off at the Boston Marathon. One of the perpetrators, Dzhokhar Tsarnaev, lay in his hospital room telling investigators bits and pieces about the attack.

Dzhokhar's older brother and mother had been on a terrorist watch list, the two brothers had reportedly been planning a second wave of attacks in New York City and the FBI [Federal Bureau of Investigation] had not ruled out the possibility of a third bomber due to the difficulty involved in detonating the bombs without a clear line of sight.

Even though Dzhokhar Tsarnaev was in no shape for a court appearance and investigators still wanted to continue questioning him under the public safety exemption of *New York v. Quarles*, a federal judge barged into the hospital room to present the charges against him and read him his rights.

There was no urgent need for a US attorney and a federal judge to rouse a terrorist listed in severe condition and read him rights. Judge Marianne Bowler's appearance in the hospital was a calculated attempt at aborting the investigation. The only reason she gave for her actions was the intense television coverage of the capture. Bowler, a [Bill] Clinton appointee, had some experience in the Muslim world and no explanation except that the case needed to move forward because it was on television.

A Disturbing Pattern

The premature Mirandizing of terrorists had become a routine practice under Attorney General Eric Holder. The Christmas Day bomber was interrogated for less than an hour before being read his Miranda rights. Like Dzhokhar, Umar Farouk Abdulmutallab was read his rights in the hospital while he was still receiving treatment.

Umar Farouk Abdulmutallab had warned that other terrorist attacks might be on the way before being read his rights. Holder took responsibility for the decision, even though Director of National Intelligence Dennis C. Blair stated that it was a mistake. A few months later, Blair was gone and Holder remained.

That year Faisal Shahzad attempted to detonate a car bomb in Times Square; an attack that the Tsarnaev brothers reportedly attempted to finish. Once again, Holder made the decision to Mirandize him. Responding to the criticism, Holder promised to seek a new exception to *Miranda* from Congress, even though he had failed to make full use of the public safety exception already in place.

Three years later, the Boston bombings show that nothing has changed. Holder has tripled down on *Miranda* even in the face of a major terrorist plot. And Holder's policy is that of an entire administration which treats terrorism as a crime and grants it the same liberal protections that criminals receive.

Protecting US Security First

[Barack] Obama could not completely dismantle the law enforcement infrastructure of the war on terror, but he did his best. The enemy combatant became the unprivileged belligerent. The [George W.] Bush administration's use of "enemy combatant" had clearly defined terrorists as members of enemy forces while the Obama administration's substitution of "unprivileged belligerent" hid their status and nature in vagueness.

Obama did his best to prevent Islamic terrorists from even being labeled "unprivileged belligerents." Obama and Holder tried to move the trial of 9/11 [referring to the September 11, 2001, terrorist attacks on the United States] mastermind Khalid Sheikh Mohammed to a civilian court. Only loud protests by New Yorkers forced a change in their plans. When Obama finally authorized the [Navy] SEALS to go after Osama bin Laden, he did so hoping to capture him and exploit the political boost to take down Guantánamo Bay [detention camp] and the use of military courts against al Qaeda terrorists.

The SEALs preempted Obama's effort to save Osama from the military court system, but he did succeed in trying Sulaiman Abu Ghaith in the civilian court system. Abu Gaith

Miranda Warning

1. You have the right to remain silent.

2. Anything you say can and will be used against you in a court of law.

3. You have the right to talk to a lawyer and have him present with you while you are being questioned.

4. If you cannot afford to hire a lawyer, one will be appointed to represent you before any questioning if you wish.

5. You can decide at any time to exercise these rights and not answer any questions or make any statements. . . .

Do you understand each of these rights I have explained to you? Having these rights in mind, do you wish to talk to us now?

"Miranda Warnings for Juveniles Clarified by Court,"
TeenJury.com, June 16, 2011.

was Osama bin Laden's son-in-law who had served as a spokesman for al Qaeda and after September 11 had threatened the United States, saying, "The planes will not stop."

Given the choice between national security and the liberal virtue of giving criminals more rights than their victims, Obama chose the latter over the former. The difference between criminals and terrorists is that a failure to get a confession from a criminal leads to a lost conviction, but a failure to extract intelligence from a terrorist can mean the deaths of hundreds or even thousands.

When the ACLU and the weight of liberal opinion stood behind Lois Ann Jameson's rapist, they were endangering countless women. The tenfold increase in rapes was largely attributable to the Left's legal and social programs. Now when they stand behind monsters like Dzhokhar Tsarnaev, they are opening the door to the Muslim rape of America, to massive acts of terror that could have been stopped and countless dead who could have been saved.

The liberal campaign for murderers and rapists covered their hands in the blood of innocents, but their campaign for terrorists will cover it in the blood of a nation.

> *"As the nearly 1,000 terrorism trials over the last decade indicate, the federal court system is well equipped to handle the complexities of terrorism cases."*

Domestic Terrorists Should Be Prosecuted in Civilian Courts

Melanie Getreuer

Melanie Getreuer is a doctoral candidate in political science at the University of Wisconsin-Madison. In the following viewpoint, she assesses the US Justice Department's policy of trying domestic terrorism suspects in civilian courts. Getreuer cites the institutional safeguards that protect classified information and the impressive track record the Justice Department has with trying domestic terrorism in civilian courts. Another advantage of the civilian court system is that domestic terrorists end up in the American prison system, which allows authorities to control the flow of information, learn valuable intelligence on terrorist activities and terrorist networks, and track released terrorists. Getreuer asserts that utilizing the criminal justice system to prosecute terrorist suspects keeps America aligned with a number of US allies, including Britain, France, Italy, and Russia.

As you read, consider the following questions:

1. According to New York University's Center on Law and Security, how many terrorism indictments on average has the US Justice Department issued per year since 2001?

2. According to the viewpoint, what is the US Justice Department's conviction rate with both domestic and international terrorist suspects?

3. What convicted domestic terrorist was the only one executed in the last two decades in the United States, according to Getreuer?

Boston Marathon bombing suspect Dzhokhar Tsarnaev is now sitting in a 10-by-10-foot cell at Federal Medical Center, Devens in Ayer, Mass. about 40 miles west of Boston. There, he awaits the next steps in the US government's case against him—first, a probable cause hearing scheduled for May 30, [2013].

A Growing Controversy

Before Mr. Tsarnaev got to this point, there was debate among some lawmakers about whether Tsarnaev should be tried as an enemy combatant in a military tribunal or whether he should be tried as a civilian in the federal court system. The arguments from those who pushed for a military trial were at best misplaced. As a US citizen, Tsarnaev could not have been tried in a military tribunal. Those arguments also ignored the institutional safeguards that already exist in our federal court system to protect classified information, as well as the impressive track record of the Justice Department in prosecuting terrorism since September 11, 2001.

As the nearly 1,000 terrorism trials over the last decade indicate, the federal court system is well equipped to handle the complexities of terrorism cases. And it is well equipped to administer justice in the case of Dzhokhar Tsarnaev. In fact, as global counterterrorism efforts have shifted to the legal arena across countries as diverse as Britain and Russia, Tsarnaev's trial can show Americans the benefits of approaching terrorism as the serious international *criminal* threat that it is, rather than as part of the so-called global "war on terror."

Europe has increasingly combated terrorism through the criminal justice system, significantly expanding laws for arresting, trying, and detaining terrorism suspects. The Tsarnaev trial may therefore help to harmonize US counterterrorism efforts with those of our closest international counterterrorism partners, while also allowing America to more effectively participate in the global counterterrorism conversation.

America's Fight Against Terrorism

The US Justice Department has proven both remarkably efficient and effective at putting terrorism on trial. As research by NYU's [New York University] Center on Law and Security shows, the Department of Justice has averaged about 30 terrorism indictments a year since 2001. (The exception to this statistic is from 2009–2010 when, on the heels of increased law enforcement sting operations and a renewed focus on extremists associated with the terrorist group Al-Shabaab, rates nearly doubled.)

Most of those trials have proceeded without the use of classified evidence, and over half have involved American citizens. Like Tsarnaev, 60 percent of these American defendants had no direct affiliation with a terrorist organization.

In choosing to charge Tsarnaev with using a "weapon of mass destruction [WMD]," the surviving Boston Marathon bombing suspect falls under an infrequently used, but widely interpreted, terrorism statute. Just 25 of all domestic terrorism cases since 2001 have involved a WMD charge. Yet the penalty has been leveled at an infamous group of confirmed and would-be terrorists, including September 11's "20th hijacker,"

Zacarias Moussaoui, shoe bomber Richard Reid, and Najibullah Zazi, the individual who plotted to plant bombs in the New York City subway system.

Almost all terrorism trials since 2001, whether of domestic or international defendants, have also ended in convictions. In fact, with a conviction rate of nearly 90 percent, it is almost certain that if Tsarnaev's case continues to the jury stage, he will be found guilty. That it will reach that point, however, is itself not guaranteed: Some two-thirds of all terrorism cases have ended in guilty plea agreements. While this is lower than the overall percentage of federal cases that end in plea agreements, coupled with the strong case against him, it suggests that the Tsarnaev trial may at least be very short.

The Implications of the Tsarnaev Case

The more interesting question in this case is what will become of Tsarnaev after his trial is completed, and what his story might mean for US counterterrorism efforts going forward. Much of the conversation since Tsarnaev was formally charged has questioned whether he will get the death penalty if he is convicted.

Given that America has executed just one convicted terrorist in the last two decades—Timothy McVeigh for the Oklahoma City bombings in 1995—it is not likely. Indeed, my own research has shown that more than half of all convicted terrorists are sitting in federal prisons in the United States (at last count, there were 400 in total), serving an average sentence of at least 14 years.

Those serving time for the most egregious terrorism crimes are in for life. Among them is the "Blind Sheikh," Omar Abdel-Rahman, who was charged with "seditious conspiracy" after an investigation of the 1993 World Trade Center bombings.

Convicted terrorists in US federal prisons have only severely restricted access to outsiders and outside information, and their activities inside prison walls are under heavy surveillance. They are also barred from significant contact with the general prison population, usually segregated from other inmates and confined to single cell blocks with single guards.

The Benefits of the Correctional Approach

This correctional approach to extremism—one that relies on the criminal justice system—echoes trends across a number of other countries, including Britain, France, Italy, and Russia, and has helped the US to gain and share valuable intelligence about terrorism. Prison officers regularly report and exchange information with global partners about the activities of these inmates.

Indeed, it was such shared information—gathered from phone calls and letters intercepted by guards—that alerted authorities to a fatwa the "Blind Sheikh" issued when he was first incarcerated that called on al Qaeda to attack the US. It was also prison intelligence that linked the 2004 Madrid train bombings to a group of al Qaeda members detained in Spanish jails after September 11. And it is prison intelligence that has in more recent years warned about the growing convergence between terrorist networks and transnational organized crime.

Moreover, both international and federal level law enforcement keeps tabs on inmates with past terrorist ties after they are released—just as these agencies do with other types of violent criminals such as pedophiles or organized crime leaders.

The fact that probation officers with the [Federal] Bureau of Prisons track formerly convicted terrorists for lengthy periods, and that they are watched closely by INTERPOL (the International Criminal Police Organization) and the FBI [Federal Bureau of Investigation], appears to have been an effective deterrent to further radicalization, as these inmates have rarely reoffended. This is an important contrast to Guantánamo [Guantánamo Bay, a US detention camp], where a full quarter

The Boston Marathon Bombing

On 15 April 2013, two bombs made from pressure cookers exploded at the Boston Marathon, killing three people, including an 8-year-old boy, and wounding at least 180 others. Authorities recovered shards of metal, wires, batteries, and fabric from the scene, and determined that the bombs were carried to the race's finishing area in black nylon bags. Because the Boston Marathon was heavily photographed and recorded, law enforcement agents had access to hundreds of hours of footage, which they examined for clues leading to the perpetrators. The day after the bombing, . . . President Barack Obama stated that "anytime bombs are used to target innocent civilians, it is an act of terror." On 18 April, the FBI [Federal Bureau of Investigation] released video and still photos of two suspects, and asked for help from the public in identifying them. In the late hours of 18 April into the early hours of the following morning, the suspects shot and killed a police officer and carjacked a Mercedes SUV. After a chase, the first suspect, Tamerlan Tsarnaev, 26, was killed in a shootout with police. His brother, Dzhokhar, 19, was wounded but escaped. A massive manhunt for Dzhokhar, the second suspect of the bombings, led to the shutdown of the entire city of Boston. Ultimately, Dzhokhar was found hiding in a boat parked in a backyard in Watertown. He was taken into custody in the evening of 19 April. Dzhokhar was charged on 22 April for using a weapon of mass destruction and malicious destruction of property. If he is convicted of the charges, he could receive the death penalty.

"Terrorism,"
Global Issues in Context *Online Collection, 2014.*

of those who have been released from incarceration there have subsequently gone on to commit or are suspected of committing further terrorist crimes.

Future Challenges

The outcome of the Tsarnaev trial, therefore, has broader implications for counterterrorism here at home and overseas. Until the marathon, America had arguably not had a major terrorist attack on US soil since September 11. This is a testament to the proactive, preventative work of international, federal, state, and local law enforcement agencies—work that has often gone unrecognized amid the race to assign blame for perceived failures and concerns over counterterrorism methods and resources.

The more important future challenge is how best to streamline the increased use of America's criminal justice system to counter terrorism with the efforts that have been developing simultaneously across the globe.

This coming summer, five high-profile terrorism suspects extradited from Britain will stand trial here in New York City for their role in the bombings of two US embassies in Africa in 1998 and for conspiring with individuals in Seattle to set up terrorist training camps inside the US. Together with the Tsarnaev trial, these cases should prompt a renewed look at counterterrorism efforts across the entire US criminal justice system to ensure that they are aligned with global trends, goals, and strategies.

> *"Whether the terrorist is foreign or do-mestic, visitor or citizen, Muslim, Christian or Jew, if he or she seeks to inflict mass casualties on Americans while in league with our enemies, they will be hunted, held and, ultimately, sentenced."*

Boston Bomber Acted as "Enemy Combatant"

Michael M. Rosen

Michael M. Rosen is an attorney and a conservative political activist. In the following viewpoint, he maintains that Dzhokhar Tsarnaev, the surviving suspect in the 2013 Boston Marathon bombing, should be classified as an enemy combatant. Rosen suggests that treating and trying domestic terrorist suspects as enemy combatants will act as a deterrent to others thinking of committing terrorist acts. Even naturalized citizens like Tsarnaev should be eligible to be regarded as enemy combatants. Rosen asserts that there are benefits to treating domestic terrorist suspects as enemy combatants, including a better chance of gleaning key intelligence and the option of trying suspects in a military tribunal instead of a civilian court.

As you read, consider the following questions:

1. According to Rosen, in what year did the US Congress expand the definition of "enemy combatant"?

2. When did Russia request further investigation of Tamerlan Tsarnaev, according to Rosen?

3. What major terrorist does Rosen report the US Congress precluded prosecuting before a civilian court?

The [Barack] Obama administration announced on Monday [April 22, 2013] that suspected Boston Marathon bomber Dzhokhar Tsarnaev would "not be treated as an enemy combatant" who would be tried in a special military tribunal. Instead, White House spokesman Jay Carney declared, "we will prosecute this terrorist through our civilian system of justice."

A Major Error

But this decision is a grave mistake for legal, political and practical reasons. As we sift through the challenging implications of last week's events, we must aim to deter future acts of terror on our soil by U.S. citizens and legal residents. Treating and trying domestic terrorists as enemy combatants can provide such a deterrent.

The strongest reason to do this is to send a signal to other would-be terrorists that we, as a society, consider these acts so repellant that we treat them as acts of war.

There are many other reasons as well. First, when overwhelming evidence indicates a suspect's guilt; when that suspect or his associates appear to have links to foreign terrorist movements; and when the crime they're accused of involves intimidating the public. Under these circumstances, it's appropriate to cite the suspect as an enemy combatant.

Enemy Combatant?

In 2006, Congress expanded the post-September 11 [referring to the September 11, 2001, terrorist attacks on the United States] definition of "enemy combatant" to mean someone "who has engaged in hostilities or who has purposefully and materially supported hostilities against the United States or its co-belligerents who is not a lawful enemy combatant (including a person who is part of the Taliban, al Qaeda or associated forces)."

There is now good reason to believe that the Tsarnaev brothers have supported hostilities against the United States and its allies. While no clear link exists yet between the suspects and radical Chechen separatists (let alone al Qaeda or the Taliban), the circumstantial evidence available to the public—including Tamerlan Tsarnaev's recent lengthy visit to the north Caucasus, his familiarity with online jihadist content and Russia's 2011 request for further investigation—suggests a connection to Islamic militants.

Even under the [Barack] Obama administration's refinement of the concept in which the Justice Department jettisoned the term "enemy combatant," Washington still has the right to detain anyone who "substantially supported" our enemies—"including any person who has committed a belligerent act or has directly supported hostilities, in aid of such enemy armed forces."

Some legal scholars and pundits, including in these pages, have argued it would be unlawful to try the remaining suspect as an enemy combatant. One writer, for example, said it would be "absolutely nuts," notwithstanding the criminal complaint filed against him Monday morning, alleging "use of a weapon of mass destruction."

What Are Military Commissions?

Military commissions are a form of military tribunal convened to try individuals for unlawful conduct associated with war. Though sometimes controversial, they are rooted in U.S. law and in the international laws of war. Foreshadowed by military tribunals convened during the American Revolution, the term "military commission" first became common in the U.S. during the Mexican-American War of the mid-19th century. Subsequent practice, legislation and U.S. Supreme Court precedents have shaped them. Today, a convening authority appointed by the U.S. secretary of defense convenes military commissions under the Military Commissions Act of 2009, passed by the U.S. Congress and signed by President Barack Obama on October 27, 2009.

"Military Commissions History,"
US Department of Justice, 2014.

The critics are correct that the standards for detaining the younger Tsarnaev, a naturalized U.S. citizen, are higher. But neither his status nor his capture on U.S. soil bars the application of combatant status.

The Benefits of an Enemy Combatant Classification

Second, treating and trying the Boston suspect as an enemy combatant confers important practical benefits. As Senators John McCain (R-Ariz.), Kelly Ayotte (R-N.H.) and Lindsey Graham (R-S.C.) have contended, eliciting information from Tsarnaev now, in the early days, is key.

"We need to know about any possible future attacks which could take additional American lives," the senators rightly proclaim. "The least of our worries is a criminal trial which will likely be held years from now."

Detaining the suspect as a belligerent would be the most effective method of gleaning key intelligence. Setting aside the legal debate about the "public safety" exception to his Miranda rights, let alone whether those rights even apply, the White House cannot keep Tsarnaev away from his attorney for much longer under ordinary criminal procedure.

By contrast, a combatant designation would, as the *Wall Street Journal* puts it, "allow for extensive, long-term interrogation without a lawyer," including "long-term psychological pressure [that] can be crucial to learning if the brothers worked with anyone else, if they received terrorist training and more."

The administration can always later reclassify Tsarnaev as a civilian suspect. Abandoning the opportunity to classify him as an enemy combatant now, however, risks losing actionable intelligence.

Military Tribunals

Trying Tsarnaev as a combatant would also relieve the severe logistical and security pressures created by a civilian trial in federal district court. Much as the Justice Department recognized when it acquiesced in Congress's wise 2011 decision to preclude trying Khalid Sheikh Mohammed and other Guantánamo Bay terrorists before civilian courts, the circus of a public trial, its potential for the revelation of sensitive intelligence and security concerns should render this a nonstarter in Boston.

While a public trial can provide catharsis for the marathon bombing survivors and their families, as the civilian trial of Zacarias Moussaoui showed—during which the 20th September 11, 2001, bomber declared "God curse America, and

God save Osama bin Laden! You will never get him!"—it can also provide terrorists with an open microphone to spout propaganda.

Moreover, while [lawyer and journalist] Daphne Eviatar has in these pages eloquently cataloged certain serious problems infecting military commissions in Guantánamo, the solution is to improve those tribunals, not to end them.

Whether the terrorist is foreign or domestic, visitor or citizen, Muslim, Christian or Jew, if he or she seeks to inflict mass casualties on Americans while in league with our enemies, they will be hunted, held and, ultimately, sentenced.

Just as we'll bring to bear the entirety of our local, state and federal law enforcement apparatus to catch a perpetrator, so too we should apply every legal weapon in our arsenal—including military tribunals—to bring them to justice.

| "Our political leaders, of all people, should champion the fact that American courts are fully able to fairly try individuals accused of even the worst crimes, up to and including acts of terrorism."

Different Standards Should Not Be Applied to Different Kinds of Domestic Terrorists

Jill Filipovic

Jill Filipovic is a journalist and political blogger. In the following viewpoint, she contends that instead of calling for some suspected domestic terrorists to be treated as enemy combatants, US politicians should recognize that the US criminal justice system is strong enough to handle the complexities of domestic terrorist trials. Filipovic argues that such demands also reveal a lack of respect for the American justice system. She notes that there is a disparity in the treatment of US domestic terrorist suspects: those motivated by extremist Christian beliefs, such as antiabortion terrorists, never have their constitutional rights questioned, and those inspired by Islamic fundamentalism are usually chal-

lenged by those who want to treat them as enemy combatants. Filipovic states that it violates American values to treat domestic terrorists differently based on factors such as religion or race.

As you read, consider the following questions:

1. According to the author, what US senator objected to the idea of treating suspected Boston Marathon bomber Dzhokhar Tsarnaev as a criminal and not as an enemy combatant?

2. How many anthrax and bioterrorism threats does the author report have been made by domestic terrorists in the United States since the late 1970s?

3. Who is Cheryl Sullenger, according to Filipovic?

When is a violent attacker a terrorist, an enemy combatant or a criminal? To some hawkish Republicans, the answer appears to depend more on a suspect's religion than his actions or affiliations.

Dzhokhar Tsarnaev, the younger of the Boston bombers, is the latest example. In allegedly carrying out the bombing at the Boston Marathon, Tsarnaev and his older brother appear to have acted alone. At the time of writing, there is no suggestion that they were affiliated with any terrorist cell or organization, let alone the army of a foreign nation. The motives behind the bombing remain unclear, but even if the surviving Tsarnaev does go on to justify the attack with religion or anti-Americanism, that doesn't meet even the intentionally loose, disturbingly Orwellian definition of "enemy combatant" outlined post-9/11 [referring to the September 11, 2001, terrorist attacks on the United States] by the [George W.] Bush administration.

The Right Decision

Given these facts, the White House made the commonsense (and legally tenable) decision to try Tsarnaev in criminal court as a civilian. But some Republican legislators aren't content with using our justice system—they want Tsarnaev to be designated an "enemy combatant," against all the available evidence.

Senator Lindsey Graham, for example, recognizes that Tsarnaev couldn't reasonably be tried by a military tribunal, but says the administration should deem him an enemy combatant nonetheless, for intelligence-gathering purposes. To clarify Senator Graham's point: He's advocating against the basic constitutional protections that the United States affords individuals accused of crimes. Doing so displays not just a disturbing level of cynicism and bigotry, but a shameful lack of respect for the American justice system and the US Constitution.

Our criminal justice system is vastly imperfect. We incarcerate more people than any nation in the history of the world, and we dole out sentences that are longer and harsher than they would be in many other countries. We've privatized the building of prisons, incentivizing more incarcerations. Our solitary confinement practices and our collective refusal to do anything about prison rape often means that incarceration crosses the line into torture.

But there are bright spots—at least, in the legal foundations of what can be a very broken system—and chief among them are our protections of the rights of the accused. It can be frustrating when there's a mountain of evidence indicating that the accused did something terrible, as there is in the Boston Marathon bombings, and we want fast and easy justice. But protections for the accused are what maintain balance in our legal system, and what allow us to instill our collective faith in it.

A Strong and Fair System

That means investigations may take longer and getting convictions may be more difficult. But that's a strength, not a weakness—a system that prioritizes quick and easy convictions is not often particularly just. A system that prioritizes a just and exhaustive process earns credibility and gains the confidence of the citizens it serves.

Our country's choice to take the lengthier but fairer path should be a point of pride.

Our political leaders, of all people, should champion the fact that American courts are fully able to fairly try individuals accused of even the worst crimes, up to and including acts of terrorism. They should champion the idea that our constitutional protections are so valuable and so fundamental to American justice that we extend them even to the worst of criminals, up to and including terrorists.

Under both George W. Bush and Barack Obama, many of our political leaders have failed on that point, as enemy combatant status has been used to hold foreign nationals indefinitely without trial. To see lawmakers attempt to score political points by suggesting that the rights of US citizens accused of perpetrating domestic attacks should be set aside if the bad guy is *really* bad is disturbing and disheartening.

Ignoring History

It's also disturbing to see how right-wing legislators define "really bad." The Tsarnaev brothers are hardly the first accused of being domestic criminals who have killed and maimed innocent bystanders in an ideologically or religiously motivated attack (assuming, even, that the Tsarnaevs acted as charged because of some broader ideology and not just because they were two angry young men with homemade bombs). Over the past few decades, thousands of acts of religiously and ideologically motivated violence have been carried out against US citizens by individuals associated with organizations that promote the use of violence to achieve their social and political goals.

Since the late 1970s, these groups have carried out eight murders, 17 attempted murders, 41 bombings, 175 arsons, 100 butyric acid attacks, 663 anthrax and bioterrorism threats, four kidnappings, 178 burglaries and 191 acts of assault and battery. At least one of them even targeted a major sporting event, setting off a bomb at the 1996 Atlanta Olympics that killed one person and injured 111 others—an attack that has now been frequently compared with the Boston Marathon bombing.

Detecting a Right-Wing Bias

But these terrorists are pro-life Christians. And typically, their attacks target abortion clinics. So there has never even been a debate about *their* constitutional rights.

Nor should there be, even though I find their views and actions odious. Right-wing terrorists deserve to be Mirandized, effectively represented and considered innocent until proven guilty—just like any other accused criminal. I do have to wonder what's wrong with a movement that accepts admitted terrorists back into its fold, as the antiabortion folks did with Cheryl Sullenger, a woman who served two years in federal prison after pleading guilty to conspiring to bomb an abortion clinic. Sullenger now works as the senior policy adviser of an antiabortion organization. But that's the "pro-life" movement's prerogative, and its particular morality.

The American criminal justice system has proven time and again that it is fully capable of trying domestic terrorists. There's little difference between the acts allegedly carried out by the Boston Marathon bombers and those committed by Eric Rudolph, the right-wing Olympic Park Bomber. It's only the religion of the bombers that seems to be motivating the very different political responses.

Protecting American Values

Does any reasonable person think we'd even be having this conversation about enemy combatant status if the Boston bombers had gone to church every Sunday or were members of a right-wing militia? Allowing the religious beliefs of the accused to sway our legal treatment of them is bigoted, deeply unjust and contrary to what we so often profess are basic American values.

Terrorism works only insofar as it terrorizes—if it instills a fear that changes our behaviors, limits our ability to live normally and chips away at our most valued institutions. "Letting the terrorists win" is a tired cliché, and I don't imagine that if we compromise our ideals and treat accused domestic terrorists as a special class to whom we afford only limited criminal defendants' rights, Dzhokhar Tsarnaev or Eric Rudolph or Khalid Sheikh Mohammed will claim victory.

But if we do follow Senator Graham's lead and agree it's acceptable to cut constitutional corners for certain kinds of bad guys, we will have ceded the integrity of our legal system, our sense of justice and our principles. Then, all of us will lose.

"It is undoubtedly true that today's war on terror falls outside the lines of traditional warfare, and perhaps we need to look at today's enemies in a new light."

Domestic Terrorists Should Be Charged with Treason

Lauren Prunty

Lauren Prunty is the managing editor of the Journal of Civil Rights and Economic Development. *In the following viewpoint, she maintains that convicted domestic terrorists should be prosecuted for treason. Prunty finds this to be more effective than passing the Terrorist Expatriation Act, which would serve to strip the citizenship of any US citizen who was accused of providing material support to a foreign terrorist organization. She argues that the Terrorist Expatriation Act violates the rights and protections afforded US citizens under the Constitution because every citizen is afforded due process under the law. Instead, she states, antiterrorism law should evolve to confront the changing nature of domestic terrorism threats and recognize that individuals who attack their homeland are committing treason and should be treated that way.*

Lauren Prunty, "Terrorism as Treason: US Citizens and Domestic Terror," *JURIST*, September 11, 2011. Courtesy of JURIST, 2011. Reproduced by permission.

As you read, consider the following questions:

1. According to Prunty, how many members of the Somali community in Minnesota were arrested and charged for providing material support to a terrorist organization in August 2010?

2. When was Hawo Mohamed Hassan scheduled to be tried in federal court on charges of conspiracy and providing material support to a terrorist organization?

3. What two US senators does Prunty identify as the co-sponsors to the Terrorist Expatriation Act?

In August 2010, Hawo Mohamed Hassan, a 63-year-old woman from Minnesota, was arrested and charged along with 13 other members of the Somali community for providing material support to a terrorist organization. Hassan went door-to-door collecting charitable donations of food, medical supplies and other necessities in an effort to bring humanitarian aid to the people of war-torn Somalia. Nonetheless, the US Department of Justice (DOJ) indicted Hassan and the others on charges of channeling funds and supplying fighters to the militant Somali group Al-Shabaab. In other words, for providing "material support" to terrorists. While Hassan has maintained that she did not know the funds were being channeled to Al-Shabaab, this is of little importance to the DOJ, as acts of terrorism can be unintentional under the [USA] PATRIOT Act, signed into law by President George W. Bush.

Under current antiterrorism statutes, "material support" is broadly defined. It does not require that the actor either intend to or know they are funding terrorism. This means that a person like Hassan can be found to materially support terrorism without ever knowing she did so. Hassan has declared her innocence. However, she has also admitted to raising the funds and, unfortunately, there is no distinction in the eyes of the law.

The Terrorist Expatriation Act

In October 2011, Hassan will face trial in a federal court on charges of conspiracy and providing material support to a terrorist organization. If she is convicted, she may face a life sentence. However, under the proposed Terrorist Expatriation Act, she could instead be subjected to an arguably more grave possibility; the recision of her US citizenship—punishment far worse than prison, without a trial or due process protections that are mandated by the Constitution.

In May 2010, Senators Joe Lieberman and Scott Brown proposed an addition to the current expatriation statute, making the provision of material support of resources to a foreign terrorist organization an action for which a US citizen may lose his or her citizenship. The proposed amendment relies on the same broad definition of material support found in the antiterrorism statutes. The bill seeks to bring existing federal law concerning expatriation up to date by including provisions applicable to the current war on terror, such as allowing the State Department to revoke the citizenship of people suspected of allying themselves with terrorist organizations. As Senator Lieberman stated, the current war on terror involves "fighting an enemy who doesn't wear the uniform of a conventional army or follow the law of war."

It is undoubtedly true that today's war on terror falls outside the lines of traditional warfare, and perhaps we need to look at today's enemies in a new light. However, it is also important to remember that today's enemies may often be US citizens, fighting against our country from within. For example, Faisal Shahzad, the Times Square bomber, planned and attempted to commit acts of war against his own country. Nonetheless, as a US citizen he was afforded the rights and protections guaranteed by the Constitution. However deplorable and reprehensible the actions of domestic terrorists may be, they are still US citizens and their constitutional rights must be honored. Otherwise, the rights and privileges of US

The Fate of Hawo Mohamed Hassan

[On May 16, 2013, in federal court,] two Rochester, Minnesota, women were sentenced for providing material support to Al-Shabaab, a U.S.-designated foreign terrorist organization. United States District Court Chief Judge Michael J. Davis sentenced Amina Farah Ali, age 36, to 240 months in federal prison, followed by supervised release for life, on one count of conspiracy to provide material support to foreign terrorist organization Al-Shabaab and twelve counts of providing material support to Al-Shabaab. Chief Judge Davis also sentenced Hawo Mohamed Hassan, age 66, to 120 months in federal prison, followed by supervised release for life, on one count of conspiracy to provide material support to a terroristic organization and two counts of making false statements to authorities. Both women, who are naturalized U.S. citizens from Somalia, were indicted on July 6, 2010, and were convicted on October 20, 2011. . . .

Evidence presented at their trial proved that the defendants provided support to Al-Shabaab from September 17, 2008, through July 19, 2009. Specifically, Ali communicated by telephone with Somalia-based members of Al-Shabaab who requested financial assistance on behalf of the group. Ali, Hassan, and others raised money for the terrorist organization by soliciting funds door to door in Somali neighborhoods in Minneapolis, Rochester, and other cities. . . . Ali often sought the money under false pretenses, contending that it was to help the poor. The defendants also obtained funds by participating in teleconferences that featured speakers who encouraged listeners to make donations in support of Al-Shabaab.

"More Terrorism Sentences Imposed in Federal Court,"
United States Attorney's Office: Minnesota, May 16, 2013.

citizenship ultimately become meaningless. Legislation that seeks to revoke an individual's citizenship before a criminal conviction, or before they are afforded a trial and due process, is quite simply unconstitutional.

The Evolution of Domestic Terrorism

Despite the changing nature of today's warfare, a domestic enemy is anything but new. Concerns regarding treason, the only crime listed in the Constitution, date back to the days of Benedict Arnold and the Founding Fathers themselves. The Constitution defines treason as an act of "levying war against the United States." Historically, during times of conventional war, an individual aiding the enemy by providing information, support or other resources would be subject to prosecution for treason. However, in the twenty-first century, questions of war and treason in the US do not involve conventional enemies. Rather, treason today takes the form of Faisal Shahzad or Farooque Ahmed, who attempted to bomb the DC Metro, and other domestic terrorists, whose actions are tantamount to waging war against the US.

If we recognize domestic terrorism as the modern-day incarnation of treason, the proposed Terrorist Expatriation Act is both redundant and unnecessary. In addition to being constitutionally invalid, the proposed subsection merely reiterates federal expatriation law that has been in place since the 1940s, and under which an individual may be stripped of their citizenship following a trial and conviction for the charge of treason. In looking at the future of both domestic and foreign policy, the US must recognize that modern-day terrorists who attack their homeland are in fact committing treason. Today's world no longer involves Benedict Arnold or Russian double agents, rather treason today has taken on the form of domestic terrorism and individuals that levy war against the US and advocate for the overthrow of the nation.

Periodical and Internet Sources Bibliography

The following articles have been selected to supplement the diverse views presented in this chapter.

Sam Finegold and Gina Kim	"Treason in the War on Terror," *Harvard Political Review*, December 7, 2011.
Jonathan Hafetz	"The Right Way to Treat a Terrorism Suspect," *The Hill*, April 24, 2013.
Craig Martin	"Boston and the Dangerous Calls for 'Enemy Combatant' Status," *Huffington Post*, April 30, 2013.
Evan Perez	"Rights Are Curtailed for Terror Suspects," *Wall Street Journal*, March 24, 2011.
Rick Perlstein	"How FBI Entrapment Is Inventing 'Terrorists'—and Letting Bad Guys Off the Hook," *Rolling Stone*, May 15, 2012.
H. Joshua Rivera	"At Least Give Them Miranda: An Exception to Prompt Presentment as an Alternative to Denying Fundamental Fifth Amendment Rights in Domestic Terrorism Cases," *American Criminal Law Review*, Winter 2012.
William Saletan	"The Miranda Warning," *Slate*, August 13, 2013.
Charlie Savage	"Debate over Delaying of Miranda Warning," *New York Times*, April 20, 2013.
Julianne Escobedo Shepherd	"Obama Curbs Miranda Rights for Domestic Terror Suspects," AlterNet, March 24, 2011.
Ishaan Tharoor	"Have We Turned a Blind Eye to Domestic Terrorism?," *Time*, August 10, 2012.
Darrel Vandeveld and Joshua Dratel	"Military Commissions: A Bad Idea," *Salon*, March 10, 2010.

For Further Discussion

Chapter 1

1. Risa Brooks argues that Americans must recognize domestic terrorism of all types, not just Muslim homegrown terrorism. Do you think focusing on terrorist threats from extremist Islamic ideologies alone makes the United States more vulnerable to domestic terrorism? Explain and give examples of other groups that pose a threat to American national security.

2. According to Scott Stewart, domestic terrorism in the United States is cyclical. What does Stewart mean by the word "cyclical"? What factors does Stewart give for the wave of violence the United States experienced in the summer of 2012?

Chapter 2

1. Peter Bergen and Jennifer Rowland claim that right-wing terrorism in the United States has recently been on the rise, while al Qaeda–inspired terrorism has declined. What reasons do the authors give for making this claim? Do you agree or disagree with their argument? Explain.

2. Jim Kouri predicts that the lone-wolf terrorist will be the most serious domestic terrorism threat to the United States in the coming years. Do you agree with Kouri? Why, or why not?

Chapter 3

1. Tim Sorrick maintains that the US intelligence community must profile potential terrorists to combat domestic terrorism. However, Elizabeth Goitein and Faiza Patel assert that profiling is an ineffective counterterrorism strategy. In your opinion, which viewpoint offers a more compelling argument, and why?

2. Toni Johnson argues that US law enforcement authorities are unable to identify potential domestic terrorists because they have a weak relationship with the Muslim community. What suggestions does Johnson offer to solve this problem? Do you think the suggestions she provides will help foster a stronger relationship between the two groups? Why, or why not?

Chapter 4

1. Emily Bazelon contends that US law enforcement officials should not be permitted to bypass Miranda rights, even for suspected terrorists. On the other hand, Daniel Greenfield asserts that reading Miranda rights to suspected terrorists is a threat to national security. In your opinion, should Miranda rights be upheld at all times, or should there be exceptions to the rule? Explain your reasoning.

2. Lauren Prunty claims that domestic terrorism is a form of treason and that convicted domestic terrorists should be prosecuted under those terms. What is Prunty's reasoning behind her argument? Do you agree or disagree? Explain.

Organizations to Contact

The editors have compiled the following list of organizations concerned with the issues debated in this book. The descriptions are derived from materials provided by the organizations. All have publications or information available for interested readers. The list was compiled on the date of publication of the present volume; the information provided here may change. Be aware that many organizations take several weeks or longer to respond to inquiries, so allow as much time as possible.

Anti-Defamation League (ADL)
605 Third Avenue, New York, NY   10158-3560
(212) 885-7700
website: www.adl.org

The Anti-Defamation League (ADL) was founded in 1913 to defend Jewish people from defamation and to ensure fairness and equality for all. Now the nation's premier civil rights and human relations agency, ADL fights anti-Semitism and all forms of bigotry, defends democratic ideals, and protects civil rights for all. As part of its efforts, ADL has taken a hard stance against domestic terrorism and works to increase awareness of the dangers of extremism through the publication of reports such as "Sovereign Citizens: A Growing Anti-Government Movement" and "Extremism in Florida: The Dark Side of the Sunshine State."

Center for Strategic and International Studies (CSIS)
1616 Rhode Island Avenue NW, Washington, DC   20036
(202) 887-0200 • fax: (202) 775-3199
website: http://csis.org

The Center for Strategic and International Studies (CSIS) is a nonprofit research organization that seeks to find bipartisan solutions to the many policy challenges faced by lawmakers on both sides of the political spectrum. Among many other issues, CSIS has devoted considerable resources toward the development of initiatives aimed at combating terrorist activities, including those of homegrown domestic terrorists, as outlined in reports such as "Homegrown Terrorism" and "A Growing Terrorist Threat?: Assessing 'Homegrown' Extremism in the United States."

Council on Foreign Relations (CFR)

The Harold Pratt House, 58 East Sixty-Eighth Street
New York, NY   10065
(212) 434-9400 • fax: (212) 434-9800
website: www.cfr.org

A nonpartisan think tank, the Council on Foreign Relations (CFR) serves as an important, informative resource for anyone seeking to learn about the challenges the United States faces in regard to foreign policy decisions. As part of its diverse range of offerings, CFR provides a wealth of information on international terrorism and all forms of domestic extremism, including reports and backgrounders such as "Militant Extremists in the United States" and "Threat of Homegrown Islamist Terrorism." In addition, CFR publishes the magazine *Foreign Affairs*.

Federal Bureau of Investigation (FBI)

935 Pennsylvania Avenue NW, Washington, DC   20535-0001
(202) 324-3000
website: www.fbi.gov

The Federal Bureau of Investigation (FBI) is a national law enforcement agency that strives to uphold national security and protect the United States and American citizens from a variety of threats, including both international and domestic terrorism. Utilizing its extensive intelligence and investigative networks, the FBI works alongside other national security organizations to neutralize terrorists and terrorist cells domestically and around the world. The FBI website provides information on domestic terrorism through reports, testimony, and articles such as "Domestic Terrorism: Focus on Militia Extremism" and "Domestic Threat: White Supremacy Extremism."

Heritage Foundation

214 Massachusetts Avenue NE, Washington, DC   20002-4999
(202) 546-4400
website: www.heritage.org

A political think tank that has been in operation since 1973, the Heritage Foundation provides lawmakers with policy ideas that reflect conservative ideals and principles. Through research and the publication of exhaustive reports, such as "60 Terrorist Plots Since 9/11: Continued Lessons in Domestic Counterterrorism" and "Terror Trends: 40 Years' Data on International and Domestic Terrorism," the Heritage Foundation's staff ensures that lawmakers have the information they need to pursue and develop contemporary conservative policies on a wide variety of important political issues, including terrorism of all kinds.

Hoover Institution

434 Galvez Mall, Stanford, CA   94305-6010
(650) 723-1754
website: www.hoover.org

The Hoover Institution at Stanford University is a public policy research organization that focuses on politics, economics, and foreign affairs. Through publications such as the *Hoover Digest* and *Defining Ideas*, as well as through research compiled by its task forces and working groups, the Hoover Institution provides information on a broad range of topics, including domestic terrorism, which the organization has addressed in reports such as "Citizen Terrorist" and "Policing Terrorism."

National Security Agency (NSA)

9800 Savage Road, Suite 6940, Fort Meade, MD   20755-6940
website: www.nsa.gov

The National Security Agency (NSA) is a government-run surveillance organization that gathers information and intelligence to thwart criminal activity and uphold public safety. The NSA's primary purpose is to use the information it gathers to prevent potential terror attacks with the help of other counterterrorism organizations. The NSA also works to protect sensitive national security information and to collect intelligence from abroad for military purposes. The NSA's quarterly magazine, the *Next Wave*, provides information on technological advancements and research activities that can help protect national security.

RAND Corporation

1776 Main Street, Santa Monica, CA   90401-3208
(310) 393-0411 • fax: (310) 393-4818
website: www.rand.org

The RAND Corporation is a policy research organization that provides lawmakers with extensive information and policy ideas for a wide variety of contemporary issues. As part of its mission to serve those who mold the nation's constantly evolving government policies, RAND offers a database of information on a wide variety of topics, including domestic terrorism, so that lawmakers can develop sound, knowledgeable solutions. This database includes in-depth reports such as "Domestic Terrorism: A National Assessment of State and Local Law Enforcement Preparedness" and "Identifying Enemies Among Us."

Southern Poverty Law Center (SPLC)

400 Washington Avenue, Montgomery, AL   36104
(334) 956-8200
website: www.splcenter.org

Since 1971, the Southern Poverty Law Center (SPLC) has been defending the most vulnerable segments of the American population from harmful effects of hate and bigotry of all sorts. Throughout its history, the SPLC has taken a hard stand against the kind of intolerance and extremism that fuels hate groups and domestic terror organizations. The SPLC gathers information on such organizations, helps law enforcement agencies in their efforts to investigate them, and assists in their prosecution. The SPLC's strategy for taking a stand against hate and extremism also includes raising public awareness through the publication of reports such as "Terror from the Right: Plots, Conspiracies, and Racist Rampages Since Oklahoma City" and "The Second Wave: Return of the Militias."

United States Department of Homeland Security (DHS)
650 Massachusetts Avenue NW, Washington, DC   20001
(202) 282-8000
website: www.dhs.gov

Founded shortly after the terrorist attacks of September 11, 2001, the United States Department of Homeland Security (DHS) is a federal agency charged with preventing future terrorist attacks and ensuring the safety and security of American citizens. Its other responsibilities include securing national borders, enforcing immigration laws, safeguarding cyberspace, and keeping the nation prepared for and capable of surviving natural disasters. The DHS website offers testimony and reports on domestic terrorism, including "How DHS Is Countering Violent Extremism" and "Partnering with Communities to Counter Violent Extremism."

United States Department of Justice (DOJ)
950 Pennsylvania Avenue NW, Washington, DC   20530-0001
(202) 514-2000
e-mail: AskDOJ@usdoj.gov
website: www.justice.gov

The United States Department of Justice (DOJ) is the primary law enforcement arm of the US government. The DOJ's Counterterrorism Section (CTS) plays a key role in the development, execution, and enforcement of various policies aimed at combating terrorism at all levels. As part of its efforts, CTS investigates and prosecutes terrorism cases, collects and analyzes data relating to terrorism, and provides information relating to domestic terrorism through the publication of related reports and testimonies, such as "Hate Crimes and the Threat of Domestic Extremism."

United States Gang Intelligence Agency (USGIA)
3509 Connecticut Avenue NW, Suite 1003
Washington, DC   20008
(202) 481-1311 • fax: (202) 481-1312
e-mail: info@usgia.org
website: www.usgia.org

A private domestic intelligence firm, the United States Gang Intelligence Agency (USGIA) works to protect the American public from mass victim related acts (MVRA). As part of its commitment to public safety, the USGIA places substantial emphasis on the prevention of domestic terrorism through the investigation and prosecution of gangs and gang members that participate in terrorist activities or otherwise contribute to such activities. The USGIA website includes a section on domestic terrorism that provides several ways the average American can help in the fight against terrorist activities.

Bibliography of Books

Eli Berman — *Radical, Religious, and Violent: The New Economics of Terrorism.* Cambridge, MA: MIT Press, 2011.

Kevin Borgeson and Robin Valeri — *Terrorism in America.* Sudbury, MA: Jones and Bartlett Publishers, 2009.

Alethia Cook — *Emergency Response to Domestic Terrorism: How Bureaucracies Reacted to the 1995 Oklahoma City Bombing.* New York: Continuum International, 2009.

Audrey Kurth Cronin — *How Terrorism Ends: Understanding the Decline and Demise of Terrorist Campaigns.* Princeton, NJ: Princeton University Press, 2009.

Mark S. Hamm — *Terrorism as Crime: From Oklahoma City to Al-Qaeda and Beyond.* New York: New York University Press, 2007.

Christopher Hewitt — *Understanding Terrorism in America: From the Klan to Al Qaeda.* New York: Routledge, 2002.

Bruce Hoffman — *Inside Terrorism.* New York: Columbia University Press, 2006.

Anna Hudson and Edwin Davidson, eds. — *Domestic Terrorism.* Hauppauge, NY: Nova Science Publishers, 2012.

Richard J. Hughbank, Anthony F. Niosi, and Juan Carlos Dumas, eds.
The Dynamics of Terror and Creation of Homegrown Terrorists. Mustang, OK: Tate Publishing & Enterprises LLC, 2010.

Daryl Johnson
Right-Wing Resurgence: How a Domestic Terrorism Threat Is Being Ignored. Lanham, MD: Rowman & Littlefield, 2012.

Douglas Kellner
Guys and Guns Amok: Domestic Terrorism and School Shootings from the Oklahoma City Bombing to the Virginia Tech Massacre. Boulder, CO: Paradigm, 2008.

Jack Levin
Domestic Terrorism. New York: Chelsea House Publishers, 2006.

Joseph T. McCann
Terrorism on American Soil: A Concise History of Plots and Perpetrators from the Famous to the Forgotten. Boulder, CO: Sentient Publications, 2006.

James F. McDonnell
Constitutional Issues in Federal Management of Domestic Terrorism Incidents. Lincoln, NE: iUniverse Inc., 2004.

Benjamin Netanyahu
Fighting Terrorism: How Democracies Can Defeat Domestic and International Terrorism. New York: Farrar, Straus and Giroux, 2001.

Peter Olsson — *The Making of a Homegrown Terrorist: Brainwashing Rebels in Search of a Cause.* Santa Barbara, CA: Praeger, 2014.

Paul Craig Roberts — *How America Was Lost: From 9/11 to the Police/Warfare State.* Atlanta, GA: Clarity Press, 2014.

Jim Rodgers and Tim Kullman — *Facing Terror: The Government's Response to Contemporary Extremists in America.* Lanham, MD: University Press of America, 2002.

Mark A. Sauter and James Jay Carafano — *Homeland Security: A Complete Guide to Understanding, Preventing, and Surviving Terrorism.* New York: McGraw-Hill, 2005.

Gary J. Schmitt, ed. — *Safety, Liberty, and Islamist Terrorism: American and European Approaches to Domestic Counterterrorism.* Washington, DC: AEI Press, 2010.

Jeffrey D. Simon — *Lone Wolf Terrorism: Understanding the Growing Threat.* Amherst, NY: Prometheus Books, 2013.

Neil J. Smelser — *The Faces of Terrorism: Social and Psychological Dimensions.* Princeton, NJ: Princeton University Press, 2007.

Erroll Southers — *Homegrown Violent Extremism.* Waltham, MA: Anderson Publishing, 2013.

Terry D. Turchie and Kathleen M. Puckett *Hunting the American Terrorist: The FBI's War on Homegrown Terror.* Palisades, NY: History Publishing Company, 2007.

Jonathan R. White *Terrorism and Homeland Security.* Belmont, CA: Wadsworth, 2013.

Index

A

F